How to Love God and
Keep His Commandments

The cover art is *The Old Testament Trinity*,
a fifteenth-century icon by the Russian
iconographer Andrei Rublev. It depicts
Abraham's encounter with God in the form of
three angels (Genesis 18-19), who represent
the Three Persons of the Trinity.

Charles Joseph
Quadrupani

How to Love God
and
Keep His
Commandments

SOPHIA INSTITUTE PRESS®
Manchester, New Hampshire

How to Love God and Keep His Commandments is an abridged edition of *Light and Peace,* published in 1912 by B. Herder, St. Louis, Missouri. This 1999 edition by Sophia Institute Press contains minor editorial revisions to the original text and replaces the introduction in the 1912 edition with the original concluding paragraphs from that edition.

On the cover: Andrei Rublev's icon *The Old Testament Trinity,* Tretyakov Gallery, Moscow, Russia (photo courtesy of Scala/Art Resource, New York).

Sophia Institute Press®
Box 5284, Manchester, NH 03108
1-800-888-9344
www.sophiainstitute.com

Nihil obstat: F. G. Holweck, *Censor Librorum*
Imprimatur: John J. Glennon, Archbishop of St. Louis
June 11, 1904

Library of Congress Cataloging-in-Publication Data

Quadrupani, Carlo Giuseppe.
  [Selections. English]
  How to love God and keep His commandments / Charles
Joseph Quadrupani.
    p. cm.
  ISBN 1-928832-02-4 (pbk. : alk. paper)
  1. Christian life — Catholic authors. I. Title.

BX2350.2.Q33 1999
248.4'82 — dc21   99-048235

99 00 01 02 03 10 9 8 7 6 5 4 3 2 1

Contents

Translator's preface. vii

Introduction xi

Part One

Practicing Your Faith

1. Be not dismayed by temptations. 5

2. Learn to pray always 15

3. Undertake penance prudently. 33

4. Learn to make fruitful confessions 39

5. Make use of wise spiritual direction 57

6. Nourish your soul with Holy Communion. 63

7. Glorify God in all you do. 75

Part Two

Developing Inner Peace

8. Hope in God's mercy 83

9. Dwell always in God's presence. 89

10. Develop a humble spirit. 93

11. Abandon yourself to God's will. 99

12. Maintain interior peace 107

13. Yield not to sadness. 113

14. Have a spirit of liberty 117

15. Strive for Christian perfection. 127

Part Three
Loving Others

16. Love God and your neighbor. 145

17. Let prudence guide your zeal 153

18. Imitate Christ's meekness. 161

19. Be charitable in conversations. 167

20. Perfect yourself step by step. 175

Biographical Note

Charles Joseph Quadrupani. 179

Translator's preface

❧

These instructions were written in 1795 by the illustrious and saintly Barnabite Father Quadrupani. They contain a summary of spiritual guidance for earnest Christians in the ordinary duties of life in the world. The author had formed his own spirituality on the model presented by the life and teaching of St. Francis de Sales,[1] and in this little book, he reflects the wisdom, prudence, and sweetness of that "gentleman saint."

The work has passed through uncounted editions in its original Italian and through a large number of editions in both the French and the German translations. The author's teaching is decidedly practical and practicable, and appeals in every way to the common sense and fits in with the busy, matter-of-fact life of the average Catholic.

The present translation has been made from the twentieth French edition and has been collated with the thirty-second edition of the original Italian published at Naples in 1818.

I. M. O'R
Overbrook, Pennsylvania

---

[1] St. Francis de Sales (1567-1622), Bishop of Geneva.

❧

Introduction

The writer of these instructions makes no pretension to have derived them from his own wisdom. The material was furnished by the greatest saints and the most eminent Doctors of the Church. You can therefore believe in them with great confidence, follow them without fear, and adopt them as a safe and reliable guide in your spiritual life.

If you try to regulate your practice by making personal and indiscriminate application of everything you find in sermons and books, you will never be at rest. One draws you to the right, the other to the left, says St. Francis de Sales; doctrine is one, but its applications are many, and they vary according to time, place, and person.

Besides, those who speak to a hardened multitude, from whom they cannot get even a little without exacting a great deal, insist vehemently upon the subject with which they wish to impress their hearers and, for the time being, appear to forget everything else. If they preach on mortification of the senses, fasting, or any other penitential work, they fail to explain the proper manner of practicing it, the limits that should not usually be exceeded, and the circumstances under which we can and should refrain from it. This is due to the fact that the cowardly and the lukewarm, whom it is more necessary to excite than to restrain, will take from these instructions only just what is suitable for them. Now, as these form the majority, it is for them above all that it is necessary to speak.

It would then be better for you individually, without lessening your respect and esteem for books of devotion and for preachers animated by the spirit of God, to confine yourself as far as practice is concerned to the advice of your spiritual director and to the teachings of the saints as presented in this little volume.

St. Francis de Sales counsels you to select your spiritual director carefully and to allow yourself subsequently to be entirely directed by him, as though he were an angel come down from Heaven to conduct you there.

Now, in observing these instructions, you will have for spiritual guide and director not the poor sinner who has compiled them for the glory of God and the good of souls, but St. Augustine,[2] St. Thomas,[3] St. Philip Neri,[4] and especially St. Francis de Sales, in whom the Church recognizes and admires such exalted sanctity, profound wisdom, and rare experience in the direction of souls. These are the three eminent qualities requisite to constitute a great Doctor in the Catholic Church and to form the safest and most enlightened guide for those who wish to be his disciples.

---

[2] St. Augustine (354-430), Bishop of Hippo.
[3] St. Thomas Aquinas (c. 1225-1274), Dominican philosopher and theologian.
[4] St. Philip Neri (1515-1595), Italian priest who founded the Congregation of the Oratory.

❧

How to Love God and
Keep His Commandments

Part One

❧

Practicing Your Faith

Editor's note: The biblical quotations in these pages are based on the Douay-Rheims edition of the Old and New Testaments. Where applicable, biblical quotations have been cross-referenced with the differing names and numeration in the Revised Standard Version, using the following symbol: (RSV =).

Chapter One

☙

Be not dismayed by temptations

"My brethren, count it all joy
when you shall fall into diverse temptations."

James 1:2

"Now, if I do that which I will not,
it is no more I that do it, but sin
that dwelleth in me."

Romans 7:20

"If we are tempted," says the Holy Spirit, "it is a sign that God loves us." Those whom God best loves have been most exposed to temptations. "Because thou wast acceptable to God," said the angel to Tobias, "it was necessary that temptation should prove thee."[5]

Do not ask God to deliver you from temptations, but to grant you the grace not to succumb to them and to do nothing contrary to His divine will. He who refuses the combat renounces the crown. Place all your trust in God, and God will Himself do battle for you against the enemy.[6]

⚭

Temptations can strengthen and purify your soul

"These persistent temptations come from the malice of the Devil," says St. Francis de Sales, "but the trouble and suffering they cause us come from the mercy of God. Thus, despite the will of the tempter, God converts his evil machinations into a distress that we may make meritorious. Therefore, I say your

[5] Tob. 12:13.

[6] St. Paul says, "God is faithful. He will not suffer you to be tempted above what you are able, but will even make with temptation issue, that you may be able to bear it" (1 Cor. 10:13).

temptations are from the Devil and Hell, but your anxiety and affliction are from God and Heaven."[7] Despise temptation, then, and open wide your soul to this suffering that God sends in order to purify you here, that He may reward you hereafter.

"Let the wind blow," remarks the same saint, "and do not mistake the rustling of leaves for the clashing of arms. Be perfectly convinced that all the temptations of Hell are powerless to defile a soul that does not love them. St. Paul endured terrible temptations, yet God, through love, did not deliver him from them."[8] Look upon God as an infinitely good and tender Father, and believe that He allows the Devil to try his children only so that their merits may increase and their recompense be correspondingly greater.

Do not confuse temptation with sin

The more persistent the temptation, the clearer it is that you have not given consent to it. "It is a good sign," says St. Francis de Sales, "when the tempter makes so much noise and commotion outside of the will, for it shows that he is not within."[9] An enemy does not besiege a fortress that is already in his power, and the more obstinate the attack, the more certain we may be that our resistance continues.

---

[7] Letter to Jane de Chantal, February 18, 1605; cf. St. Francis de Sales, *Thy Will Be Done* (Manchester, New Hampshire: Sophia Institute Press, 1995), 210.

[8] Cf. Letter to Jane de Chantal, August 28, 1605; *Thy Will Be Done*, 213, 214-215.

[9] Letter to Jane de Chantal, February 18, 1605; cf. *Thy Will Be Done*, 209.

Be not dismayed by temptations

Your fears lead you to believe you are defeated at the very moment you are gaining the victory. This comes from the fact that you confound feeling with consent, and, mistaking a passive condition of the imagination for an act of the will, you consider that you have yielded to the temptation because you felt it keenly.

St. Francis de Sales, with his usual simplicity, thus describes this warring of the flesh against the spirit:

> You are right, my dear daughter. There are two women within you . . . and the two children of these different mothers quarrel, and the good-for-nothing one is so bad that sometimes the good one can scarcely defend herself, and then she takes it into her head that she has been worsted and that the wicked one is braver than she. Now, surely, this is not true. The bad one is not the stronger by any means, but only slyer, more persistent, and more obstinate. When she succeeds in making you weep, she is delighted, because that is always just so much time lost, and she is content to make you lose time when she cannot make you lose eternity.

It is not always in our power to restrain the imagination. St. Jerome[10] had retired into the desert, and still his fancy represented to him the dances of the Roman ladies. His body was benumbed, as it were, and his blood chilled by the severity of his mortifications, and yet the flames of concupiscence encompassed and tortured his heart. During these frightful conflicts, the holy anchorite suffered, but he did not sin; he was

[10] St. Jerome (c. 342-420), biblical scholar.

tormented, but was not guilty; on the contrary, his merits were augmented in the sight of God in proportion to the intensity of the temptations.

The holy abbot St. Anthony[11] was wont to say to the phantoms of his mind, "I see you, but I do not look at you; I see you because it does not depend upon me that my imagination places before my eyes things I would wish not to see; I do not look at you because with my will I repulse and reject you." "It is so much the essence of sin to be voluntary," says St. Augustine, "that if not voluntary, it is not sin."

The attraction of the feelings toward the object presented by the imagination is at times so strong that the will seems to have been carried away and overcome by a sort of fascination. This, however, is not the case. The will suffered, but did not consent; it was attacked and wounded, but not conquered. This state of things coincides with what St. Paul says of the revolt of the flesh against the spirit and of their unceasing warfare.[12] The soul, indeed, experiences strange sensations, but as it does not consent to them, it passes through the ordeal unsullied, just as substances coated with oil may be immersed in water without absorbing a single drop of it.

St. Francis de Sales explains this distinction so plainly and yet so simply in one of his letters, that it may be useful to repeat the passage here:

Courage, my dear soul; I say it with great love in Jesus Christ, dear soul, courage! As long as we can exclaim resolutely, even though without feeling, "My Jesus!" there

[11] St. Anthony (251-356), hermit.

[12] Cf. Rom. 7:14-23.

is no cause for alarm. Do not tell me it appears to you that you say it in a cowardly way, and only by doing great violence to yourself. It is precisely this holy violence that bears away the kingdom of Heaven. Do you not see, my daughter, it is a sign that the enemy has taken everything within our fortress except the impenetrable, unconquerable tower? — and that can never be lost save by willful surrender. This tower is the free will, which, perfectly visible to the eye of God, occupies the highest and most spiritual region of the soul, dependent on none but God and oneself; and when all the other faculties are lost and in subjection to the enemy, it alone remains free to give or to refuse consent.

Now, you often see souls afflicted because the enemy, occupying all the other faculties, makes therein so great a noise and confusion that they scarcely can hear what this superior will says; for although it has a clearer and more penetrating voice than the inferior will, the loud, boisterous cries of the latter almost drown it. But note this well: as long as the temptation is displeasing to you, there is nothing to fear; for why should it displease you, except because you do not will it?[13]

Find peace of conscience through spiritual obedience
If it frequently happens that you have not a distinct consciousness of your success against temptation, it may be that

[13] Letter to Jane de Chantal, February 18, 1605; cf. *Thy Will Be Done*, 209-210.

How to Love God and Keep His Commandments

God refuses you this satisfaction in order that, lacking this clear assurance, your knowledge may come through obedience. Therefore, when your spiritual director, after hearing your explanation, says that you have not given consent, you should be satisfied with his decision and abide by it with perfect tranquillity, discarding all fear that he did not understand you aright or that you did not explain the matter sufficiently. These doubts are but fresh artifices of the Devil to rob you of the merit of obedience. As has been said above, to give way to such disquietude is to offend seriously against this virtue, for all direction would thus be rendered impossible, by the failure of the penitent to recognize God Himself in the person of his director.

To constitute a mortal sin, three conditions must coexist. First, the matter must be weighty; second, the mind must have full knowledge of the guilt of the action, omission, or dangerous occasion in question; and, third, the will, through a criminal preference for the forbidden action, culpable omission, or proximate occasion of sin, must give full consent. These reflections should serve to reassure your mind if the fear of having committed a mortal sin disturbs it, for it is very difficult for this threefold union of conditions to be effected in a God-fearing soul.

However, perfect security can come, and ought to come, only from spiritual obedience.

Turn peacefully away from temptations
In temptations against faith or against purity, do not make great efforts to form acts of these virtues, but simply turn a pleading glance toward God, without speaking even to this

compassionate Friend concerning the thought that afflicts you, lest thereby you root the evil suggestion more firmly. Then, without disquieting yourself, engage at once in some exterior occupation or continue what you were doing. Make no answer to the tempter, but ignore him, just as though his assault had never occurred. In this way, while preserving your own peace of soul, you will cover your enemy with confusion.

The same counsel is given by St. Francis de Sales in his characteristic style: "Do you know how God acts on these occasions? He permits the wicked maker of such wares to come and offer them to us for sale, in order that by the contempt we show for them, we may testify our love for holy things. And for this, is it necessary, my dear child, to feel anxious and to change our position? No, no. It is only the Devil who is prowling around your soul, raging and storming, to see if he can find an open door. . . . What! And you would be annoyed at that? Let the enemy storm away; only be careful on your part to keep all the entrances well fastened, and finally he will grow weary; or if he does not, God will force him to raise the siege."[14]

Even if you should be assailed by temptations during your entire lifetime, do not be disquieted, for your merits will increase in proportion to your trials and your crown will be accordingly all the brighter in Heaven. The only thing necessary is to remain firm in your resolution to despise the efforts of the tempter.

This serious trial, and so many others that have assailed you and left you troubled in mind do not at all surprise

---

[14] Letter to Jane de Chantal, February 18, 1605; cf. *Thy Will Be Done*, 208-209.

me, since there is nothing worse. Do not worry, then, my beloved daughter. Should we allow ourselves to be swept away by the current and the storm? Let Satan rage at the door; he may knock and stamp, and clamor and howl, and do his worst, but rest assured that he can never enter our souls but through the door of our consent. Let us only keep that closed tight and often look to see that it is well secured, and we need have no concern about all the rest — there is no danger.[15]

The most learned theologians and masters of the spiritual life agree in saying that simply to ignore a temptation is a much more effectual means to repulse it than words and acts of the contrary virtues.

⇢

Suggestions for
further reading:

St. Francis de Sales, *Introduction to the
Devout Life*, Part 4, chs. 3, 4

Lorenzo Scupoli, *The Spiritual Combat*, ch. 12

Thomas à Kempis, *Imitation of Christ*,
Bk. 3, chs. 6, 7, 12, 20, 29, 55, 57

---

[15] St. Francis de Sales, Letter to the Abbess of Puits d'Orbe, April 1605; cf. St. Francis de Sales, *Letters to Persons in Religion* (Westminster, Maryland: The Newman Bookshop, 1943), 58.

Chapter Two

Learn to pray always

"Who can persevere the whole day
in the praise of God? I will suggest a help.
Whatsoever thou doest, do well,
and thou hast praised God."

St. Augustine, *Discourse 2 on Psalm 34*

"Oh! what do I suffer interiorly whilst with my mind
I consider heavenly things and presently a crowd
of carnal thoughts interrupts me as I pray."

Thomas à Kempis, *Imitation of Christ*, Bk. 3, ch. 48, no. 5

We ought to love meditation and should make it often on the Passion of our divine Lord, striving above all to derive therefrom fruits of humility, patience, and charity.

※

Do not be dismayed by dryness in prayer

If you experience great dryness in your meditations or other prayers, do not feel distressed and conclude that God has turned His face away from you. Far from it.

Prayer said with aridity is usually the most meritorious. Yet it is quite a common error to confound the value of prayer with its perceptible results, and the merit acquired with the satisfaction experienced. The facility and sweetness you may have in prayer are favors from God, for which you will have to account to Him; hence, the result is not merit but debt.[16] The very fact that we derive less gratification from such prayer makes it all the more pleasing to God, because we are thus suffering for love of Him. Let us call to mind at such times that our Lord prayed without consolation throughout His bitter agony.[17]

---

[16] Cf. *Imitation of Christ*, Bk. 2, ch. 9.
[17] Matt. 26:38-45.

How to Love God and Keep His Commandments

"All this trouble comes from self-love and from the good opinion we have of ourselves," says St. Francis de Sales. "If our hearts do not melt with tenderness, if we have no relish or perceptible feeling in prayer, if we do not enjoy great interior sweetness during meditation, we are at once overwhelmed with sadness. If we find difficulty in doing good, if some obstacle is opposed to our pious designs, we give way to disquietude and are eager to conquer all this and to be free from it. Why? Undoubtedly because we love consolations, our own comfort, our own convenience. We wish to pray immersed in sweetness and to be virtuous, that we may eat sugar; and we do not contemplate our Savior Jesus Christ, who, prone upon the ground, is covered with a sweat of blood caused by the intense conflict He feels interiorly between the repugnances of the inferior portion of His soul and the resolutions of the superior."[18]

The same teaching is given by another great master of the spiritual life:

> We frequently seek the gratification and consolation of self-love in the testimony we desire to render to ourselves. Thus, we are disturbed about our lack of sensible fervor, whereas in reality we never pray so well as when we are tempted to think we are not praying at all. We fear to pray badly then, but we should fear rather to give way to the vexation of our cowardly nature, to a philosophical infidelity, which ever wishes to demonstrate to itself its own operations in fine, to an impatient desire to see and to feel in order to console ourselves.

[18] Letter to the Abbess of Puits d'Orbe, April 1605; cf. *Letters to Persons in Religion*, 59.

There is no penance more bitter than this state of pure faith without sensible support. Hence, I conclude that it is freer than any other from illusion. Strange temptation — to seek impatiently for sensible consolation through fear of not being sufficiently penitent! Ah, why not rather accept as a penance the deprivation of that consolation we are so tempted to seek?[19]

If you have an ardent desire for the perceptible love of God, a desire that cannot but be pleasing to Him, provided you are at the same time resigned to be deprived of it, remember that according to St. John Chrysostom,[20] it can be obtained only by fidelity to prayer. God wishes, says the saint, to make us realize by experience that we cannot have His love except from Him, and that this love, which is the true happiness of our souls, is not to be acquired by the reflections of our minds or the natural efforts of our hearts, but by the gratuitous infusion of the Holy Spirit. Yes, this love is so great a good that God wishes to be the sole dispenser of it: He bestows it only in proportion as we ask it of Him and ordinarily makes us wait for some time before He grants it.

You will sometimes imagine that at prayer your soul is not in the presence of God and that only your body is in the church, like the statues and candelabras that adorn the altars. Think, then, that you share with those inanimate objects the honor of serving as ornaments for the house of God, and that

---

[19] Cf. François Fénelon (1651-1715; Archbishop of Cambrai), *Spiritual Progress,* ed. James W. Metcalf (New York: M. W. Dodd, 1853), "Christian Counsel," ch. 7.

[20] St. John Chrysostom (c. 347-407), Bishop of Constantinople.

in the presence of your Creator, even this humble role should seem glorious to you.

> You tell me that you cannot pray well. But what better prayer could there be than to represent to God again and again, as you are doing, your nothingness and misery? The most touching appeal beggars can make is merely to expose to us their deformities and necessities. But there are times when you cannot even do this much, you say, and that you remain there like a statue. Well, even that is better than nothing. Kings and princes have statues in their palaces for no other purpose than that they may take pleasure in looking at them; be satisfied, then, to fulfill the same office in the presence of God, and when it so pleases Him, He will animate the statue.[21]

Do not let distractions trouble you

Prepare yourself for prayer by peaceful recollection, and begin it without agitation or uneasiness. St. Francis de Sales has this to say on the subject:

> Some little time before you are going to pray, calm and compose your heart, and be hopeful of doing well; for if you begin without hope and already devoid of relish, you will find it difficult to regain an appetite. . . . The disquiet you experience in prayer, accompanied by great

---

[21] St. Francis de Sales, Letter to Madame Brulart, March 1605; cf. *Thy Will Be Done*, 187.

eagerness to discover some object that can fix and satisfy your thoughts, is of itself sufficient to prevent you from finding what you seek. When a thing is searched for with too great eagerness, one may have his hands or his eyes almost upon it a hundred times and yet fail to perceive it. This vain and useless anxiety in regard to prayer can result in nothing but weariness of mind, and this in turn produces coldness and apathy in your soul.[22]

Begin your prayer with the desire of being very recollected. This is all that is necessary. "A desire has the same value in the sight of God as a good work," says St. Gregory the Great,[23] "when the accomplishment of it does not depend upon our will." During these involuntary distractions, God withdraws the sensible feeling of His presence, but His love remains in the depths of our hearts. St. Teresa,[24] in the midst of dryness and distractions, was wont to say, "If I am not praying, I am at least doing penance." I should say you are doing both the one and the other: you do penance by all that you are suffering, and you pray by the desire and intention you have to do so.

When you have not consciously or voluntarily yielded to distractions, do not stop to find what may have been their cause, or to discover whether you have in any way given occasion to them. This would be simply to weary and disquiet yourself unprofitably. From whatever direction distractions come,

---

[22] *Letters to Persons in Religion*, 400-401; Letter to Mademoiselle de Soulfour, 1605-1608; cf. *Thy Will Be Done*, 25-26.

[23] St. Gregory I (c. 540-604), Pope from 590.

[24] St. Teresa of Avila (1515-1582), Carmelite nun and mystic.

you can convert them into a source of merit by casting yourself into the arms of the Divine Mercy.

St. Francis de Sales, when asked how he prayed, replied, "I cannot say it too often: I receive peacefully whatever the Lord sends me. If He consoles me, I kiss the right hand of His mercy; if I am dry and distracted, I kiss the left hand of His justice." This method is the only good one, for as the same saint says, "He who truly loves prayer loves it for the love of God, and he who loves it for the love of God wishes to experience in it nothing but what God is pleased to send him." Now, whatever you may experience in prayer is precisely what God wills.

Merely being in God's presence is a form of prayer

St. Francis de Sales teaches us that merely to keep ourselves peacefully and tranquilly in the presence of God, without other desire or pretension than to be near Him and to please Him, is of itself an excellent prayer, "Do not exhaust yourself," he says, "in making efforts to speak to your dear Master, for you are speaking to Him by the sole fact that you remain there and contemplate Him."[25]

> Remember that the graces and favors of prayer do not come from earth but from Heaven and therefore that no effort of ours can acquire them, although, it is true, we must dispose ourselves for their reception diligently, yet withal humbly and tranquilly. We ought to keep

[25] Letter to Mademoiselle de Soulfour, 1605-1608; cf. *Thy Will Be Done*, 27.

our hearts wide open and await the blessed dew from Heaven.

The following consideration should never be forgotten when we go to prayer — namely, that we draw near to God and place ourselves in His presence principally for two reasons. The first is to render to God the honor and the homage we owe Him, and this can be done without God speaking to us or we to Him, for the duty is fulfilled by acknowledging that He is our Creator and we are His vile creatures, and by remaining before Him, prostrate in spirit, awaiting His commands. The second reason is to speak to God and to listen to Him when He speaks to us by His inspirations and the interior movements of grace. . . .

Now, one or the other of these two advantages can never fail to be derived from prayer. If, then, we can speak to our Lord, let us do so in praise and supplication; if we are unable to speak, let us remain in His presence notwithstanding, offering Him our silent homage. He will see us there, our patience will touch Him, and our silence will plead with Him and win His favor. Another time, to our utter astonishment, He will take us by the hand, and converse with us, and make a hundred turns with us in His garden of prayer. And even should He never do this, still let us be content to know it is our duty to be in His retinue, and that it is a great favor and a greater honor for us that He suffers us in His presence.

In this way, we do not force ourselves to speak to God, for we know that merely to remain close to Him is as useful, nay, perhaps more useful to us, although it may be less to our liking. Therefore, when you draw near to our Lord, speak to Him if you can; if you cannot, stay there, let Him see you, and do not be anxious about anything else. . . . Take courage, then. Tell your Savior you will not leave Him even should He never grant you any sensible sweetness; tell Him that you will remain before Him until He has given you His blessing.[26]

The same saint gives further valuable advice as follows: "Many persons fail to make a distinction between the presence of God in their souls and the consciousness of this adorable presence, between faith and the perceptible feeling of faith. This shows a great want of discernment. When they do not realize God's presence dwelling within them, they suppose He has withdrawn Himself through some fault of theirs. This is an ignorant and hurtful error. A man who endures martyrdom for love of God does not think actually and exclusively of God but much of his own sufferings; and yet the absence of this feeling of faith does not deprive him of the great merit due to his faith and the resolutions it caused him to make and to keep."

Do not overburden yourself in prayer

Your vocal prayers should be few in number, but said with great fervor. The strength derived from food does not depend upon the quantity taken but upon its being well digested. Far better one Our Father or one psalm said with devout attention

---

[26] Cf. Letter to Mademoiselle de Soulfour, 1605-1608; *Thy Will Be Done*, 26-27.

than entire rosaries and long offices recited hurriedly and with restless eagerness.

While saying vocal prayers — aside from those of obligation — if you feel that God invites you to meditate, gently and promptly follow this divine impulse. You may be sure that in doing so, you make an exchange most profitable to yourself and agreeable to God, from whom the inspiration comes.

Be careful not to overburden yourself with too many prayers, either mental or vocal. As soon as you feel uncontrollable weariness or distaste, postpone your prayers, if possible, and seek relief in some pleasant pastime, or conversation, or in any other innocent diversion. This advice is given by St. Thomas and other learned Fathers of the Church and is of the utmost importance. Follow it conscientiously, for lassitude of mind begets coldness and a kind of spiritual stupor.

St. Teresa's opinion is that the body should be in a comfortable position when we pray, as otherwise it is difficult for the mind to pay proper attention to prayer and to God's presence. So do not fatigue your body by remaining too long prostrate or kneeling. The important thing is that the soul should humble itself before God in sentiments of respect, confidence, and love.

Never repeat a prayer, even if you have said it with many distractions. You cannot imagine the innumerable difficulties in which you may become entangled by the habit of repeating your prayers. Therefore, I beg of you not to do it.

In St. Ignatius's[27] time, there was a certain religious of the Society of Jesus who was a victim of this kind of scruple. The

----

[27] St. Ignatius of Loyola (1495-1556), founder of the Society of Jesus.

recital of the daily Office always kept him much longer than was necessary, because he would repeat again and again and for hours at a time any passage that he suspected had not been said with sufficient attention. St. Ignatius tried to correct him by various means, but in vain. At length, the thought occurred that one scruple might be cured by another. He therefore commanded the poor Jesuit, under pain of sin and in virtue of religious obedience, to close his breviary every day at the end of a specified time, this being just enough to allow him to read the Office through once and rather quickly. The first day, the religious was obliged to stop before he had half finished. This caused him such intense regret that before long, the fear of not being able to say the entire Office made him contract the habit of finishing it within the allotted time.

You should never repeat a prayer nor a point in your meditation, even if you have had in the inferior portion of your soul ideas and feelings at variance with the words pronounced by your lips or with the sentiments you wished to excite in your heart. Nay, do not be induced to do it even if these ideas and feelings are injurious to God. Under such conditions, be careful not to give way to anxiety and agitation, and do not try to make reparation for an imaginary offense. Continue your prayer in peace, as if nothing had disturbed it, not taking the trouble to notice these dogs that come from the Devil and that can bark around you while you pray, in order to distract you, if may be, but that cannot bite you unless you let them.

This temptation should be treated exactly the same as temptations of the flesh: do not dispute with it at all; rather, imitate the children of Israel who made no attempt to break the bones of the paschal lamb but cast them into the fire. You need not answer the enemy, nor even pretend to hear what he says. Let the wretch clamor at the door as much as he wants to; it is not even necessary to call, "Who is there?"

"What you tell me is no doubt true," you say, "but he annoys me, and the uproar he makes prevents those within from hearing one another speak." That makes no difference. Have patience, prostrate yourself before God, and remain at His feet. He will understand from your very attitude, although you utter no words, that you are His and that you crave His help. Above all, however, keep yourself well within, and do not on any account open the door, either to see who it is or to drive the importunate fellow away. Eventually he will tire of shouting and will leave you in peace.[28]

St. Augustine says that the Devil is a formidable giant to those who fear him, but only a miserable dwarf to those who despise him.

Gently recall your mind from distractions
Should it happen that the whole time given to prayer be passed in rejecting temptations or in recalling your mind from its wanderings, and you do not succeed in giving birth to a single devout thought or sentiment, St. Francis de Sales is authority for saying that your prayer is nevertheless all the more

---

[28] St. Francis de Sales, Letter to Jane de Chantal, October 14, 1604; cf. *Thy Will Be Done*, 230-231.

meritorious from the fact of its being so unsatisfactory to you. It makes you more like to our divine Lord when he prayed in the Garden of Gethsemani and on Mount Calvary. "Better to eat bread without sugar, than sugar without bread. We should seek the God of consolations, not the consolations of God; and in order to possess God in Heaven, we must now suffer with Him and for Him."[29]

"When your mind wanders or gives way to distractions," says St. Francis de Sales, "gently recall it and place it once more close to its divine Master. If you should do nothing else but repeat this during the whole time of prayer, your hour would be very well spent and you would perform a spiritual exercise most acceptable to God."[30]

ॐ

Pray amid your daily tasks

It is good to bear in mind that in commanding us to pray always, our Savior did not mean actual prayer, as that would be an impossibility. The desire to glorify God by all our actions suffices for the rigorous fulfillment of this precept, if this desire be habitual and permanent. "You pray often," says St. Augustine, "if you often have a desire to pay homage to God by your actions; you pray always if you always have this desire, no matter how you may be otherwise employed."

"Need we be surprised that St. Augustine often assures us that the whole Christian life is but one long, continual tending of our hearts toward that eternal justice for which we sigh

---

[29] Cf. *Introduction to the Devout Life*, Part 4, ch. 13.
[30] Cf. *Letters to Persons in Religion*, 401.

here below?" says Fénelon. "Our only happiness consists in ever thirsting for it, and this thirst is in itself a prayer; consequently, if we always desire this justice, we pray always. Do not think it necessary to pronounce a great many words and to struggle much with oneself in order to pray. To pray is to ask God that His will may be done, to form some good desire, to raise the heart to God, to long for the riches He promises us, to sigh over our miseries and the danger we are in of displeasing Him by violating His holy law. Now, this requires neither science nor method nor reasoning; one can pray without any distinct thought; no headwork is necessary; only a moment of time and a loving effusion of the heart are needed; and even this moment may be simultaneously occupied with something else, for so great is God's condescension to our weakness that He permits us to divide it when necessary between Him and creatures. Yes, during this moment, you can continue what you were doing; it is sufficient to offer to God your most ordinary occupations, or to perform them with the general intention of glorifying Him. This is the continual prayer required by St. Paul . . . thought by many devout persons to be impracticable, but in reality very easy for those who know that the best of all prayers is to do everything with a pure intention, and frequently to renew the desire to perform all our actions for God and in accordance with His divine will."

You should never omit or neglect the duties of your state of life in order to say certain self-imposed prayers. These duties are a substitute for prayers and are equally efficacious, St. Thomas teaches, for obtaining the graces you stand in need of and which are promised to those who ask for them properly. It is even more meritorious to perform some work for the love of

God, to whom we offer it, than merely to raise the soul to Him by actual prayer.

St. Francis de Sales says this: "Every person is bound to observe strictly the duties of his particular calling. Whoever fails to do this, even if he should raise the dead to life, is guilty of sin and, should the sin be grave, deserves damnation if he dies therein. For example, bishops are obliged to make a visitation of their diocese in order to console and instruct their flock and to rectify whatever may be amiss. If I, a bishop, neglect this duty, I shall be lost even if I spend my entire time in prayer and fast all my life."[31]

⁂

Make use of aspirations

Make frequent use of short and loving aspirations that raise the soul to its Creator. According to St. Francis de Sales, aspirations can, in case of necessity, replace all other prayers, whereas all other prayers cannot supply for the omission of aspirations. "Acquire the habit of making frequent aspirations. They are sighs of love that dart upward to God. . . . It will greatly facilitate this custom if you keep in mind the point of your morning's meditation that you liked best and ponder it over during the day. In sickness, let pious aspirations take the place of all other prayers."[32]

Aspirations can be made at all times, wherever we are or whatever we may be doing. They might be compared to those

---

[31] St. Francis de Sales, Letter to Madame Brulart, October 13, 1604; cf. *Thy Will Be Done*, 7.

[32] *Introduction to the Devout Life*, Part 2, ch. 13.

aromatic pastilles, which we may always have about us and take from time to time to strengthen the stomach and please the palate. Aspirations have a similar effect on the soul by refreshing and fortifying it.

The monks of old, of whom St. Augustine speaks, could not say long prayers, obliged as they were to earn their bread by daily toil. Aspirations, therefore, took the place of all others for them, and it may be said that, although laboring unceasingly, they prayed continually.

I cannot too earnestly urge you to accustom yourself to the profitable and easy practice of making aspirations. It is far preferable to saying many other vocal prayers, for, when too numerous, these are apt to employ the lips only rather than to reanimate and enlighten the soul.

⚘

Suggestion for
further reading:

Introduction to the Devout Life, Part 2, ch. 13

Chapter Three

Undertake penance prudently

"A sacrifice to God is an afflicted spirit;
a contrite and humble heart, O God,
Thou wilt not despise."

Psalm 50:19
(RSV = Psalm 51:17)

⚘

According to the teaching of St. Thomas, there are three ways of doing penance: fasting, prayer, and almsgiving, either corporal or spiritual. Therefore, you must not suppose that you are prevented from doing penance when you are not allowed to subject your body to severe fasts and painful mortifications. The other two penitential works, prayer and almsgiving, can, in this case, take the place of corporal austerities in the fulfillment of the Christian duty of penance. Observe also that it is not in accordance with the spirit of the laws of God and of His Church, which prescribe fasting, to injure your health thereby, nor to hinder the accomplishment of the duties of your state of life.

Labor, sickness, disappointments, reverse of fortune, dryness in prayer — all these, when accepted with resignation, are penitential works and are the more agreeable to God for their being so distasteful to us.

All virtues may be divided into two classes: active and passive. The characteristic of the active virtues is to do good; of the passive, to endure evil. Now, the virtues of the second class are more meritorious and less perilous. In the active virtues, nature can have a large share, and a dangerous self-complacence, or satisfaction in their effects, may easily glide into them. This danger is less to be feared in the practice of the passive virtues, especially when the sufferings are not of our own choosing but come to us directly from the hand of God.

⚜

Be modest in your penances

St. Jerome teaches that when the Devil cannot turn a soul away from the love of virtue, he tries to urge it to excessive mortification, in order that it may thus become exhausted and lose the vigor indispensable to its spiritual progress. Numbers of devout people have fallen into this snare.

"I charge you," says St. Francis de Sales, "to preserve your health carefully, for God exacts this of you, and to husband your strength so as to employ it in His service. It is even better to save more than the requisite amount of strength than to reduce it too much, for we can always lessen it at will, whereas, once lost, it is no easy matter to regain it." Therefore, give your body the nourishment it needs to maintain its strength and health.

We learn from Cassian[33] and St. Thomas that, in a celebrated conference held by the holy Abbot St. Anthony with the most learned religious of Egypt, it was decided that, of all virtues, moderation is the most useful, as it guards and preserves all the others. It is owing to the lack of this essential moderation in their devotional exercises and mortifications that many persons, while seeking holiness, find only ill health. As a consequence, they eventually abandon the path of perfection, judging it impracticable because they have attempted to walk in it bound with fetters.

---

[33] John Cassian (c. 360-435), monk.

St. Augustine makes the following apt comparison, which you can look upon as a good rule in this matter: "The body is a poor invalid confided to the charity of the soul, the soul being commissioned to give it such assistance as it requires. Hunger, thirst, and fatigue are its habitual ailments; let the soul, then, charitably apply to them the needful remedies, provided these be always within the bounds of moderation and prudence." He who acts in this way fulfills a duty of obedience to his Creator.

From these various opinions, it is easy to see how false are certain maxims met with in some ascetical works; for example, that it is of small consequence if one should shorten his life by ten or fifteen years in order to save his soul. If this were true, a much surer way would be to secure a still speedier death, and see to what that would lead. No, it is not permissible in ordinary practice to impose upon ourselves arbitrarily any kind of mortification that would directly tend to shorten life. "To kill oneself with a single blow," says St. Jerome, "or to kill oneself little by little — I make but slight distinction between these two crimes." Life, health, and strength are blessings that have been given us in trust, and we cannot lawfully dispose of them as though they belonged to us absolutely.

Do not imitate the saints'
extraordinary penances
The example of those saints who practiced extraordinary penances deserves our sincere admiration, but it is not in these exterior acts that we should try to imitate them; to do this would necessitate being as holy as they were. Duplicate their miracles also, then, if you can.

"If we had to copy the saints in everything they did," says St. Jane Frances de Chantal,[34] "it would be necessary to spend our life in a horrible cave like St. John Climacus, or on top of a pillar as St. Simeon Stylites did, to live several weeks without other nourishment than the Holy Eucharist as St. Catherine of Siena did, or to eat but a single ounce of food each day as St. Aloysius did."[35] Desires to imitate the saints in what is extraordinary are the effect of secret pride and not of genuine virtue.

The French translator of these instructions had a conversation in Rome with the learned and pious Jesuit, Fr. Rozaven, on this subject. Speaking of the extraordinary fasts and mortifications of St. Ignatius, Fr. Rozaven said, "Do not let us confound cause and effect. It is not because he did these things that Ignatius became a saint; on the contrary, it is because he was already a saint that it was possible and permissible for him to do them."

Suggestion for
further reading:

Introduction to the Devout Life, Part 3

---

[34] St. Jane Frances de Chantal (1572-1641), foundress of the Order of the Visitation.

[35] St. John Climacus (c. 570-c. 649), ascetic and spiritual writer; St. Simeon Stylites (c. 390-459), the first of the Stylites, Christian solitaries who lived on top of pillars; St. Catherine of Siena (c. 1347-1380), Dominican tertiary; possibly St. Aloysius Gonzaga (1568-1591), patron saint of Roman Catholic youth. — ED.

Chapter Four

Learn to make fruitful confessions

"I said, 'I will confess against myself my
injustice to the Lord,' and Thou hast
forgiven the wickedness of my sin."

Psalm 31:5
(RSV = Psalm 32:5)

"But if any man sin, we have an advocate
with the Father: Jesus Christ the Just."

1 John 2:1

"Whose sins you shall forgive, they are
forgiven them; and whose sins you shall
retain, they are retained."

John 20:23

The sacrament of Penance is a sacrament of mercy. We should therefore approach it with confidence and in peace.

St. Francis de Sales assures us that for those who go to Confession once a week, a quarter of an hour is enough for the examination of conscience, and a still shorter time for exciting contrition. Not even this much is necessary, he adds, for those who confess more frequently.

You need not remember
all your sins in Confession

Faults omitted in Confession, either because they were forgotten or because they seemed too trivial to mention, are nevertheless effaced by the absolution. St. Francis de Sales has this to say on the subject:

> You must not feel worried if you cannot remember all your sins when preparing for Confession, for it is incredible that anyone who often examines his conscience would overlook or be unable to recall such faults as are important. Neither should you be so keenly anxious to mention every minute imperfection, every trifling fault; it is enough to speak of these to our Lord, with a sigh

of regret and a humble heart, whenever you remark them.[36]

You must not be so anxious to tell everything, nor to run to your superiors to make a great ado over each little thing that troubles you and that will, perhaps, be forgotten in a quarter of an hour. We must learn to bear with generosity these trifles, which we cannot remedy, for ordinarily they are only the consequences of our imperfect nature. That your will, feelings, and desires are so inconstant; that you are at one time moody, at another cheerful; that you now have a wish to speak and presently feel the greatest aversion to do so; and a thousand similar insignificant matters are infirmities to which we are naturally prone and will be subject to as long as we live.[37]

St. Francis de Sales says further, "It is needless to accuse yourself in Confession of those fleeting thoughts that, like gnats, swarm around you, or of the disgust and aversion you feel in the observance of your vows and devotional exercises, for these things are not sins; they are only inconveniences, annoyances."

Rest assured that the more closely you examine your conscience, the less you will discover that is worth the trouble of telling. Moreover, you must remember that too long an examination of conscience fatigues the mind and cools the fervor of the heart.

---

[36] Conference 18; cf. St. Francis de Sales, *The Spiritual Conferences* (London: Burns and Oates, 1906), 355.

[37] Conference 14; cf. *The Spiritual Conferences*, 275.

Learn to make fruitful confessions

✿

Be specific in your confessions

To those who in their confessions are inclined to confuse involuntarily movements with sins, St. Francis de Sales gives the following useful advice:

You tell me that when you have experienced a strong feeling, you are always uneasy if you do not confess it. When you are not sure that you have given consent to it, I assure you, it is unnecessary to mention it except maybe in spiritual conference, and then not by way of accusation, but to obtain advice on how to behave another time in like circumstances. For if you say, "I accuse myself of having had movements of violent anger for two days, but I did not give way to them," you are telling your virtues, not your sins. "A doubt comes into my mind, though, that I may have committed some fault during the temptation." You must consider maturely whether this doubt has any foundation in fact and, if so, speak of the matter in Confession with all simplicity; otherwise it is better not to mention it, as you would do so only for your own satisfaction. Even should this silence cost you some pain, you must endure it as you would any other to which you can apply no remedy.[38]

"Omit from your confessions" — we again quote the same saint — "those superfluous accusations which so many persons make merely through habit: 'I have not loved God sufficiently,'

---

[38] Conference 5; cf. *The Spiritual Conferences*, 86-87.

'I have not prayed with enough fervor,' 'I have not loved my neighbor as much as I should,' 'I have not received the sacraments with all the reverence due to them,' and others of a like nature. You will readily see the reason for this. It is that, in speaking thus, you tell nothing particular that would make known to the confessor the state of your conscience, and the most perfect man living, as well as all the saints in Paradise, might say the same things were they making a confession."[39]

Those who go to Confession frequently should always bear in mind what the saintly director says in addition: "We are not obliged to confess our venial sins, but if we do so, it must be with a firm resolution to correct them; otherwise it is an abuse of the sacrament to mention them."[40]

⚜

Be at peace after Confession

After Confession, keep your soul in peace, and be on your guard — this is a point of cardinal importance — against giving access to any fear about the validity of the sacrament, as regards the examination of conscience, the contrition, or anything else whatsoever. These fears are suggestions of the Devil, whose aim it is to instill bitterness into a sacrament of consolation and love.

"After confession is not the time to examine ourselves to find if we have told all our sins. We should rather remain attentively and in peace near our Lord, with whom we have just been reconciled, and thank Him for His great mercy. Nor is it

---

[39] *Introduction to the Devout Life*, Part 2, ch. 19.
[40] Ibid.

necessary subsequently to search out what we may have forgotten. We must tell simply all that comes to mind; after that, we need think no more about it."[41]

Work calmly to overcome your sins
It is essential to be sorry for our sins; it is not essential to be troubled about them. Repentance is an effect of love of God; anxiety is an effect of self-love. In the midst of the keenest and most sincere repentance, we can still thank God that He has not permitted us to become yet more culpable. Let us promise Him a solid amendment, relying for success solely upon the assistance of divine grace; and if we should fall again a hundred times a day, let us never cease to renew the promise and the hope. God can in an instant raise up children to Abraham from the very stones[42] and exalt the most corrupt natures to the highest degree of sanctity. At times He does so, but usually it is His will that we long continue to bear the burden of our infirmity. Let us not, then, lose our trust in Him, nor mistake a state of trial for a state of reprobation.

God has, indeed, on some occasions cured sinners instantaneously and without leaving in them any trace of their previous maladies. Such, for instance, was the case with Mary Magdalene. In a moment, her soul was changed from a sink of corruption into a wellspring of perfection, never again to be contaminated by sin. But,

[41] Conference 14; cf. *The Spiritual Conferences*, 275.
[42] Cf. Matt. 3:9.

on the other hand, in several of the beloved disciples, this same God allowed many marks of their evil inclinations to remain for some time after their conversion, and this for their greater good. Witness St. Peter, who, even after the divine call, was guilty of various imperfections and once fell totally and miserably by the triple denial of his Lord and Master.

Solomon says there is no one more insolent than a servant who has suddenly become mistress.[43] A soul that after a long slavery to its passions should in a moment subjugate them completely would be in great danger of becoming a prey to pride and vanity. This dominion must be gained little by little, step by step; it cost the saints long years of labor to acquire it. Hence the necessity of having patience with everyone, but first of all with yourself.[44]

There is no sight more pleasing to Heaven than to witness the persevering and determined struggle of a soul that remains united to God by a sincere desire and a firm resolution not to offend Him, and maintaining this struggle calmly and patiently even when it is to all appearance fruitless. Such a soul, resigned to retain its defects if it is God's will, yet determined notwithstanding to fight against them relentlessly, is more precious in the eyes of God than if the practice of virtue were easy for it and it were in peaceful possession of spiritual gifts.

---

[43] "By three things is the earth disturbed . . . by a bondwoman, when she is heir to her mistress" (Prov. 30:21, 23).

[44] Letter to Madame Brulart, March 1605; cf. *Thy Will Be Done*, 186.

Labor, then, in the presence of your heavenly Father; struggle on with strength and courage; but do not be too desirous of success, for when this craving for self-satisfaction is excessive, it is sure to be accompanied by vexation and impatience. "Evil things must not be desired at all," says St. Francis de Sales, "nor good things immoderately." And elsewhere he says, "I entreat of you: love nothing too ardently, not even the virtues, for these we sometimes forfeit by exceeding the bounds of moderation."[45] And again: "Why is it that if we happen to fall into some imperfection or sin, we are surprised at ourselves and become disquieted and impatient? Undoubtedly it is because we thought there was some good in us, and that we were resolute and strong. Consequently, when we find this is not the case, that we have tripped and fallen to the earth, we are anxious, annoyed, and troubled; whereas, if we realized what we truly are, in place of being astonished at seeing ourselves down, we should wonder rather how we ever remain erect."[46]

"We should labor, therefore, without any uneasiness as to results. God requires efforts on our part, but not success. If we battle with perseverance, undaunted by our defeats, these very defeats will be worth as much to us as victories, and even more. But beware: there is a rock here! If this conflict is not undertaken in perfectly good faith, we will try to deceive ourselves as to the genuineness of our efforts by calling the cowardice

---

[45] Letter to Madame Brulart, June 10, 1605; cf. *Thy Will Be Done*, 20.

[46] Letter to the abbess of Puits d'Orbe, April 1605; cf. *Letters to Persons in Religion*, 59-60.

that caused us to refuse the battle a defeat and by dignifying with the name of trial the results of our weakness and sloth."

Contrition does not require a feeling of sorrow

Contrition is essentially an act of the will by which we detest our past sins and resolve not to commit them in future. Hence, sighs, tears, and perceptible sorrow are not necessary elements of true contrition. Contrition can even attain that degree of disinterested perfection which suffices for the justification of a sinner, in the midst of the greatest dryness and an apparent insensibility. Therefore, never allow yourself to be disturbed by the want of perceptible sorrow.

Do not make violent efforts to excite your soul to contrition, for these only have the effect of producing anxiety, weariness, and oppression of mind. On the contrary, seek to become very calm; say lovingly to God that you wish sincerely you had never offended Him and that with the assistance of His grace, you will never offend Him more. That is contrition. True contrition is a product of love, and love acts serenely.

"An act of contrition," says St. Francis de Sales, "is the work of a moment." Cast a rapid glance at yourself to see and detest your sins, and another toward God to promise Him amendment and to express a hope of obtaining His assistance in keeping this promise. David, one of the most contrite penitents who ever lived, expressed his act of contrition in a single word: *Peccavi* — "I have sinned" — and by that one word, he was justified.[47]

---

[47] 2 Kings 12:13 (RSV = 2 Sam. 12:13).

"You ask how an act of contrition can be made in a short time," says St. Francis de Sales. "I answer that a very good one can be made in almost no time. Nothing more is needed than to prostrate oneself before God in a spirit of humility and of sorrow for having offended Him."[48]

You say you wish to have contrition but cannot succeed in feeling it. St. Francis de Sales replies, "The ability to wish is a great power with God, and you thus have contrition by the simple fact that you wish to have it. You do not feel it indeed at the moment, but neither do you see or feel a fire covered with ashes; nevertheless the fire exists." The immoderate desire of perceptible sorrow comes from self-love and self-complacency. A sorrow that satisfies only God is not sufficient for us; we wish it to satisfy us also. We like to find in our sensibility a flattering and reassuring testimony of our love of good.

If God does not grant you the enjoyment of perceptible sorrow, it is in order that you may gain the merit of obedience, which should suffice to reassure you as to your perfect reconciliation. Believe, therefore, with humility, obey with courage, and you will earn a twofold reward. The greatest saints have at times believed they had neither contrition nor love, but in the midst of this darkness of the understanding, their will followed the torch of obedience with heroic submission.

Do not be surprised when you fall into the same sins
Do not conclude that you lack contrition or that your confessions are defective because you fall again into the same

---

[48] Conference 18; cf. *The Spiritual Conferences*, 355-356.

faults. It is very essential to make a distinction in regard to relapses. Those that are the offspring of a perverse will that has preserved an affection for certain venial sins, and takes pleasure and wishes to take pleasure in them, should not be tolerated; we must vigorously attack them at the very root and not allow ourselves any respite until they are utterly exterminated. But those relapses that proceed from inadvertence, from surprise notwithstanding constant vigilance, from the infirmity and frailty of our nature — to these we shall remain partially subject until our last breath.

"It will be doing very well," says St. Francis de Sales, "if we get free of certain faults a quarter of an hour before our death." And elsewhere: "We are obliged to bear not only with the failings of our neighbor, but likewise with our own and to be patient at the sight of our imperfections." We must try to correct ourselves, but we should do it tranquilly and without anxiety.

You complain that you still have many faults and failings notwithstanding your desire for perfection and a pure love of God. I assure you that it is impossible to be entirely divested of self while we are here below. We shall always be obliged to bear ourselves about with us until God transfers us to Heaven; and while we do this, we carry something that is of no value. It is necessary, therefore, to have patience, and not to expect to cure ourselves in a day of the numerous bad habits contracted through past carelessness in regard to our spiritual welfare. Pray, do not look here, there, and everywhere. Look only at God and yourself; you will never see God devoid of goodness, nor yourself without wretchedness, and that wretchedness the object of God's goodness and mercy.[49]

Fénelon speaks in the same tone:

You should never be surprised or discouraged at your faults. You must bear with them patiently, yet without flattering yourself or sparing correction. Treat yourself as you would another. As soon as you find that you have committed a fault, make an interior act of self-condemnation, turn to God to receive a penance, and then tell your fault with simplicity to your director. Begin over again to do well as though it were the first time, and do not grow weary if you have to make a fresh start every day. Nothing is more touching to the Sacred Heart of Jesus than this humble and patient courage. We should not be cast down if we have many temptations and even commit numerous faults. "Virtue," says the apostle, "is made perfect in infirmity."[50] Spiritual progress is effected less by perceptible devotion, relish, and spiritual consolations than by means of interior humiliation and frequent recourse to God.

Habitually add to your confession some general accusation of all the sins of your past life, or of such of them as occasion you the most remorse. Say, for example, I accuse myself of sins against purity, or charity, or temperance. You thus preclude

---

[49] Cf. St. Francis de Sales, Letter to Madame Brulart, March 1605; *Thy Will Be Done*, 186; *Imitation of Christ*, Bk. 3, ch. 20.
[50] 2 Cor. 12:9.

the possibility of there being lack of sufficient matter for the validity of the sacrament.

Do not fear that your confessions are not valid

Banish from your mind the dread of having omitted any sins in either your general or ordinary confessions, or of not having explained their circumstances clearly enough. The learned theologian Janin sets forth the following rules on the subject: The Church, the interpreter of the will of Jesus Christ, requires sacramental integrity in Confession, and not material integrity. The former consists in the confession of all the sins we can remember after a sufficient examination, the duration of which should be regulated by the actual state of the conscience. Material integrity would require a rigorously complete accusation of all the sins we have committed with their number and circumstances, without the slightest omission. Now, sacramental integrity may be reasonably exacted, since it exceeds no one's ability, while material integrity, on the contrary, could not be exacted without the sacrament becoming an impossibility; for, no matter how carefully we make our examination of conscience, some sin or some detail in regard to number or circumstance will always escape us. In a word, all that the Church demands of the faithful is a sincere and humble avowal of every sin that can be brought to mind after a suitable examination of conscience; for the rest, she intends good will to supply for any defect of memory.

Do not be uneasy because you fail to remember all your failings in order to tell them in Confession. This is unnecessary, because, as you often fall almost without being aware of it, so you often get up again without perceiving it. "Just as it is not said that the just man sees or feels himself fall seven times a day, but simply that he falls seven times a day,[51] in like manner, he gets up again without noticing particularly that he has done so. Hence, have no anxiety about this, but frankly and humbly confess whatever you remember, and commit the rest to the tender mercies of Him who puts His hand under those who fall without malice, so that they may not be bruised, and raises them up again so gently and swiftly that they scarcely realize they had fallen."[52]

By a diligent examination of conscience, you have thoroughly satisfied all the requirements for sacramental integrity; therefore banish whatever doubts and fears may come to beset you, for they are nothing but temptations.

If you suspect that you failed to fulfill these requirements owing to not having been particular enough about your examination of conscience, you may feel sure that your confessor has by prudent interrogations supplied for whatever may have been wanting on your part. And if he did not question you further, it was due to the fact that he understood clearly enough the nature of your sins and the state of your soul, and this is the object of sacramental accusation.

How great, then, is the error of those poor souls who wish continually to make their general confessions over again, through fear either of incomplete examination or of insufficient sorrow; and how blameworthy the weak complaisance of

---

[51] Prov. 24:16.
[52] Cf. Jean Pierre Camus, *The Spirit of St. Francis de Sales* (London: Burns and Oates, 1910), 373.

those confessors who offer no opposition to their doing so! If such fears were to be listened to, everyone would be obliged to pass his entire life in making and repeating general confessions, for they would incessantly spring up afresh, and even the greatest saints would not be exempt from them. A sacrament of consolation and love would thus be transformed into a perfect torture for the soul — a heretical perversion anathematized by the Council of Trent.

> If you really omitted something that ought to have been told, consider whether you did so consciously and voluntarily, in which case, if it was a mortal sin or you thought it one at the time, you would undoubtedly have to make the confession over again. But if it were only a venial sin or, although it was mortal, you omitted it out of forgetfulness or some defect of memory, have no scruples; for at my soul's peril, I assure you there is no obligation to repeat your confession. It will be quite sufficient to mention the matter to your ordinary confessor. I will answer for this.[53]

It is the teaching of the saints and Doctors of the Church that when a general confession has been made with a sincere and upright intention and with a desire to change one's life, the penitent should remain in peace in regard to it and not make it over again under any pretext whatsoever. Those who do otherwise recall to their memory things that should be banished from it and increase the trouble of their soul by too eager

---

[53] St. Francis de Sales, Letter to Madame Brulart, October 13, 1604; cf. *Thy Will Be Done*, 5-6.

a desire to purify it. For, as St. Philip Neri so well expresses it: the harder we sweep, the more dust we raise.

Remember, in conclusion, that according to the common opinion of the saints, the fear of sin is no longer salutary when it becomes excessive.

Chapter Five

�֍

Make use of wise spiritual direction

"For it is not you who speak,
but the Holy Spirit."
Mark 13:11

∿

When choosing a spiritual director, be careful to select a priest who has the necessary qualifications. He should be not only virtuous, but prudent, charitable, and learned. St. Francis de Sales gives the following opinion on the subject:

> "Go," said Tobias to his son, when about to send him into a strange country, "go, seek some wise man to conduct you."[54] I say the same to you. If you sincerely desire to enter upon the way of devotion, seek a good guide to direct you therein. This advice is of the utmost importance and necessity. Whatever one may do, says the devout Teresa of Avila, he can never be certain of fulfilling God's will, unless he practices that humble obedience that the saints so strongly recommend and to which they so faithfully adhere. And the Scriptures tell us, "A faithful friend is a strong defense, and he that hath found him hath found a treasure. . . . A faithful friend is the medicine of life and immortality, and they that fear the Lord shall find one."[55]
>
> But who can find such a friend? They that fear God, the wise man answers — that is to say, those humble

[54] Tob. 5:4.
[55] Ecclus. 6:14, 16.

souls who ardently desire their spiritual progress. Since it is so essential, then, to have a skillful guide in the devout life, ask God fervently to give you one according to His heart, and rest assured that when an angel is necessary to you, as to the young Tobias, He will give you a wise and faithful director.

In fact, the selection once made, you should look upon your spiritual guide more as a guardian angel than as a mere man. You place your confidence not in him but in God, for it is God who will lead and instruct you through his instrumentality by inspiring him with the sentiments and words necessary for your guidance. Thus, you may safely listen to him as to an angel sent from Heaven to lead you there. To this confidence, add perfect candor. Speak quite frankly, and tell him unreservedly all that is good and all that is evil in you, for the good will thus be strengthened, the evil weakened, and your soul shall thereby become firmer in its sufferings and more moderate in its consolations.

Great respect should also be united with confidence, and in such nice proportion that the one shall not lessen the other; let your confidence in him be such as a respectful daughter reposes in her father, your respect for him such as that with which a son confides in his mother. In a word, this friendship, although strong and tender, should be altogether sacred and spiritual in its nature.

"Choose one among a thousand," says Teresa of Avila; among ten thousand, rather, I should say, for there are fewer than one would suppose fitted for this office of spiritual director. Charity, learning, and prudence are indispensable to it, and if any one of these qualities be absent, your choice will not be unattended with danger. I repeat, ask God to inspire your selection, and when you have made it, thank Him sincerely, and then remain constant to your decision. If you go to God in all simplicity and with humility and confidence, you will undoubtedly obtain a favorable answer to your petition.[56]

In conclusion, it may be good to remind you that the director and the confessor do not necessarily have to be the same priest. St. Francis de Sales was the spiritual director of many persons to whom he was not the ordinary confessor. "To a director," he says, "we should reveal our entire soul, whereas to a confessor we simply accuse ourselves of our sins in order to receive absolution for them."

---

[56] *Introduction to the Devout Life*, Part 1, ch. 4.

Chapter Six

Nourish your soul
with Holy Communion

"Unless you eat the flesh of the Son of Man,
and drink His blood, you shall not have life in you."

John 6:54
(RSV = John 6:53)

"And if I send them away fasting . . .
they will faint in the way."

Mark 8:3

࿈

Frequent Communion is the most efficacious of all means to unite us to God. "He that eateth my flesh," said our divine Savior "abideth in me and I in him."[57]

St. Bernard[58] calls the Holy Eucharist the love of loves. Hence you should desire to receive it frequently in order to be filled with this divine love.

࿈

Holy Communion heals
and strengthens you

St. Francis de Sales says there are two classes of persons who should often receive Holy Communion: "the perfect, to unite themselves more closely to the Source of all perfection, and the imperfect, to labor to attain perfection; the strong, that they may not become weak, and the weak, that they may become strong; the sick, that they may be cured, and those in health, that they may be preserved from sickness.

"You tell me that your imperfections, your weakness, and your littleness make you unworthy to receive Communion frequently, and I assure you it is precisely because of these that

---

[57] John 6:57 (RSV = John 6:56).

[58] St. Bernard (1090-1153), Abbot of Clairvaux.

you ought to receive it frequently, in order that He who possesses all things may give you whatever is wanting to you."[59]

The Rev. Fr. Margottet, a Jesuit, took great pleasure in conversing with a certain young man who visited him regularly to be instructed and edified by his pious discourse. One day, this young man confided to him the confusion he felt in availing himself of his director's permission to receive Holy Communion several times a week. This was due especially to the thought that St. Aloysius, while a novice of the Society of Jesus, went to Communion on Sundays only. "Come, come, my dear sir," laughingly replied the good Father, "continue your frequent Communions. You need them much more than St. Aloysius did."

It is indeed an error to consider Holy Communion a reward of virtue and, in a measure, a gauge of perfection, whereas it is above all a means to attain perfection, and the one pre-existing virtue required in order to employ this means is the desire to profit by it. Our divine Lord did not say, "Come to me, all you who are perfect." He said, "Come to me, all you who labor and are burdened."[60]

The spirit of the Church has at all times been the same in regard to this important subject. Fénelon says in his letter on frequent Communion that St. Chrysostom admits of no medium between the state of those who are in mortal sin and that of the faithful who are in a state of grace and communicate every day. In vain certain Christians, believing themselves purified and just, do no penance as sinners and nevertheless

---

[59] *Introduction to the Devout Life*, Part 2, ch. 21.

[60] Matt. 11:28.

abstain from Communion, because, they say, they are not perfect enough to receive it. This intermediate state is not only most dangerous for one who willfully remains in it, but is also injurious to the Blessed Sacrament. Far from doing honor to the Holy Eucharist by depriving ourselves of it, we offend our divine Lord when we decline to partake of the banquet to which He invites us. In a word, according to this early Father of the Church, we ought either to communicate with those who are in a state of grace, or to do penance so that we may be united to them as soon as possible.

Other Fathers of the Church speak in the same way of Holy Communion: "If it is daily bread," says St. Ambrose,[61] "receive it every day in order that every day you may benefit by it. Live in such a manner that you may deserve to receive it every day, for he who does not deserve to receive it every day will not deserve to receive it at the end of the year. . . . Do you not know that every time the Holy Sacrifice is offered, the death, Resurrection, and Ascension of our Lord are renewed to the atonement of sin? And yet you will not partake daily of this Bread of Life! When one has received a wound, does he not seek a remedy? Sin, which holds us captive, is our wound; our remedy is in this ever adorable Sacrament."

In order that it may be plainly proved that the faithful of the present day have no reason to act differently in this respect from those of the primitive Church, let us see how this ancient discipline has been confirmed in later times by the Council of Trent: "Christians should believe in this Sacrament and reverence it with such a firm faith, with so much

---

[61] St. Ambrose (c. 339-397), Bishop of Milan.

fervor and piety, that they may often receive this Supersubstantial Bread; that it may be, in truth, the life of their soul and the perpetual health of their spirit, and that the strength they derive therefrom may enable them to pass from the temptations of this earthly pilgrimage to the repose of their heavenly fatherland. . . . The Council would have the faithful receive Communion each time they assist at Mass, not only spiritually, but sacramentally, that they may derive more abundant fruit from the Holy Sacrifice."

The evening before your Communion, devote some little time to recollection in order to ponder the inestimable gift that God is about to bestow upon you, and endeavor also to excite in your soul the desire and the hope of finding therein your delight.

⚭

Communion's benefits may
remain imperceptible to you

Do not conclude that you derive no benefit from Holy Communion because you find no perceptible increase in your virtues. Consider that it at least serves to keep you in a state of grace. You give nourishment to your body every day, but you do not pretend to say that it daily gains in strength. Does food appear useless to you on that account? Certainly not, for, although it fails to augment strength, it preserves it by repairing the constant waste. Now, this is precisely the case with the divine Food of our souls.

Observe, moreover, that there is no real increase in virtue without a corresponding growth in humility. Consequently, the more virtuous you are, the less so you will esteem yourself;

the worthier you are to approach your God, the more profoundly will you feel your unworthiness. For man, no matter to what degree of virtue he attains, cannot be otherwise than weak and sinful here below, and he realizes his baseness more and more distinctly in proportion to his advancement in grace and in light.

Fénelon speaks as follows on the same subject: "Hitherto you lacked the light to discover in your soul many movements of our malicious and depraved nature, which now begin to reveal themselves to you. In proportion as light increases, we find ourselves more corrupt than we supposed; but we should be neither surprised nor discouraged, for it is not that we are in reality worse than we were — on the contrary, we are better — but, while our sinfulness decreases, the light which shows it to us increases."[62]

Be not dismayed by a lack of love for Communion

A cause of frequent error and trouble, particularly in regard to Holy Communion, is that feelings are confused with acts of the will. The faculty of willing is the only one we possess as our own, the only one we can use freely and at all times. Hence, it follows that it is by the will alone that we can in reality acquire merit or commit sin. The natural virtues are gratuitous gifts of God. The world is right in esteeming them, for they come from Him, but it errs when it esteems them exclusively, for they do not of themselves give us any title to Heaven. God has placed them at the disposal of our will as means to an end, and

---

[62] Fénelon, *Spiritual Progress*, ch. 16.

we can make a good or bad use of them just as we can of all God's other gifts. We may be deprived of these natural virtues and live by the will alone, spiritually dry and devoid of sentiment and yet in a state of intimate union with God.

This explanation is intended to reassure such persons as are disposed to feel anxious when they find nothing in their hearts to correspond with the effusions of perceptible love with which books of devotion abound in the preparation for Holy Communion. These usually make the mistake of taking for granted the invariable existence of sentiment, and of addressing it exclusively. How many souls do we see who in consequence grow alarmed about their condition, believing they are devoid of grace, notwithstanding their firm will to shun sin and to please God! They should, however, not give way to anxiety, nor exhaust themselves by vain efforts to excite in their hearts a sensibility that God has not given them. When He has granted us this gift, we owe Him homage for it as for all others; but God only requires that each of His creatures should render an account of what he has received, and free will is the one thing that has been accorded indiscriminately to all men.

Thus, we find St. Francis de Sales, who possessed in such a high degree perceptible love of God and all the natural virtues, making this positive declaration: "The greatest proof we can have in this life that we are in the grace of God is not perceptible love of Him, but the firm resolution never to consent to any sin, great or small."

So do not fear that you are ill-prepared for Holy Communion and abuse the sacrament because, in receiving it, you are cold, indifferent, and devoid of feeling. This is a trial sent or permitted by God to test your faith and to advance you in merit. All that has been said in regard to dryness in prayer might be repeated here. Try to have an abiding desire to feel for the Blessed Eucharist as ardent transports of love as were ever experienced by the saints. A desire is equivalent before God to the thing desired, as I have already quoted for you from St. Gregory the Great; therefore, you should be satisfied with this when you can attain nothing higher. Everything over and above this is grace, not merit.

Receive Communion even when you feel unworthy

If you dare not receive Holy Communion often because you are not worthy, then you must never receive it, for you will never be worthy. What creature could be worthy to receive God? Moreover, to follow out this principle, we would have to abandon the practice of visiting churches and of speaking to God in prayer, for a miserable, sin-stained human being is unfit to enter the house of the Lord or to converse with Him.

"How many scrupulous Christians do we see languishing for want of this divine Food!" says Fénelon. "They consume themselves with subtle speculations and sterile efforts, they fear, they tremble, they doubt, and they vainly seek for a certainty that cannot be found in this life. Sweetness and unction are not for them. They wish to live for God without living by Him. They are dry, feeble, exhausted; they are close to the Fountain of Living Water and yet allow themselves to die of thirst. They desire to fulfill all exteriorly, yet do not dare to nourish themselves interiorly; they wish to carry the burden of the law without imbibing its spirit and its consolation from prayer and frequent Communion!"

In regard to Holy Communion, therefore, do not confine yourself to a consideration of your own unworthiness, but temper this with the thought of God's mercy. The guests at the symbolic marriage feast, a figure of the Holy Eucharist, were not the great and the rich, but the poor, the blind, and the lame. Whosoever is clothed in the nuptial garment — that is to say, whosoever is in a state of grace — is welcome to this banquet.[63]

✺

Make use of spiritual Communions

St. Francis de Sales says that when we cannot go to Holy Communion without giving annoyance to others, or without failing against duties of charity, justice, or order, we should be satisfied with spiritual Communion. "Believe me," he adds, "this mortification, this deprivation, will be extremely pleasing to God and will advance you greatly in His love. We must sometimes take a step backward in order to leap the better."[64]

It was not by frequent Communion that the holy anchorites sanctified themselves, but by the exact observance of the duties of their calling. St. Paul the Hermit[65] received Holy Communion only twice during his long, penitential life; nevertheless he was precious in the sight of God. Apropos of this subject, St. Francis de Sales gives us this admirable advice: "In proportion as you are hindered from doing the good you

---

[63] Cf. Luke 14:16-23; Matt. 22:2-13.

[64] Letter to Madame Brulart, October 1606; cf. *Thy Will Be Done*, 60-61.

[65] St. Paul of Thebes (died c. 340), first Christian hermit.

desire, do all the more ardently the good that you do not desire. You do not like to make such-and-such an act of resignation; you would prefer to make some other; but offer the one you do not like, for it will be of far greater value."[66]

St. John the Baptist was more intimately united in spirit with our Lord than even the Apostles themselves, yet he never became one of His followers, owing to the fact that his vocation required this sacrifice on his part and called him elsewhere. This is the greatest act of spiritual mortification recorded in the lives of the saints.

"I have often admired the extreme resignation of St. John the Baptist, who remained so long in the desert, quite near to our Lord, without going to see, hear, and follow Him. And after baptizing Jesus, how could he have allowed Him to depart without uniting himself to Him with His bodily presence, as he was already so united to Him by the ties of affection? Ah! the divine Precursor knew that, in his case, the Master was best served by deprivation of His actual presence. . . . It will be the same with you in regard to Holy Communion. I mean that, for the present, God will be pleased if, in accordance with the wish of the superiors whom He has placed over you, you endure the privation of His actual presence. It will be a great consolation to me to know that this advice does not disquiet your heart. Rest assured that this resignation, this renunciation, will be exceedingly beneficial to you."[67]

---

[66] Letter to Madame Brulart, October 1606; cf. *Thy Will Be Done*, 62.

[67] Letter to Madame Brulart, October 1606; cf. *Thy Will Be Done*, 60.

How to Love God and Keep His Commandments

Communion will help you resist temptations

Never refrain from receiving the Holy Eucharist because you happen to be beset by temptations; this would be to capitulate to your enemy without offering any resistance. The more combats you have to sustain, the greater the necessity of providing yourself with means of defense, and these are to be found in the Blessed Sacrament. Go courageously, then, and renew your strength with the Food of the strong, and victory shall be yours.

Suggestions for
further reading:

Introduction to the Devout Life, Part 2, chs. 20, 21

Imitation of Christ, Bk. 4, chs. 10, 16

Chapter Seven

⸕

Glorify God in all you do

"The Sabbath was made for man,
and not man for the Sabbath."

Mark 2:27

⚓

Every day of our life should be employed in glorifying God, but there are certain days He has particularly appointed whereon to receive from us a more special exterior worship. These are Sundays and holy days.

It is therefore obligatory for us to sanctify such days. The ordinary means of fulfilling this duty are, principally, the Holy Sacrifice of the Mass, the sacraments, sermons, religious instructions, works of charity, and spiritual reading.

Nevertheless, we should avoid overfatiguing the mind and wearying the body by too many exercises of devotion. Excess even in holy things is wrong, as virtue ends where excess begins. All that was said on this subject in the chapter on prayer is equally applicable here.

Moreover, it is good to know that a friendly visit, a walk, or a lawful diversion, all of which can be referred to God, serves also for the sanctification of Sundays and holy days, when undertaken with a view to please Him. The same may be said of such daily occupations as are required of man by his bodily needs.

"How often we are mistaken in our point of view!" says St. Francis de Sales. "I tell you once again: it is not the outward aspect of actions that we must look at, but their interior spirit — that is to say, whether or not they are according to the will of

God. By no means regard the nature of the things you do, but rather the honor that accrues to them, worthless as they are in themselves, from the fact that God wishes them, that they are in the order of His Providence and disposed by His infinite wisdom. In a word, if they are pleasing to God, and recognized as being so, to whom should they be displeasing?"

Be flexible in regard to your devotions

These things are said for the instruction of those who are eager and anxious on Sundays and holy days of obligation to heap devotion upon devotion and who make a crime of everything that is not an exterior act of piety. They apply themselves, it seems, to the material observance of the Sabbath, following the superstitious custom of the Pharisees instead of peacefully sanctifying the Lord's day with that sweet and holy liberty of spirit which our divine Savior teaches in the Gospel. Too much dissipation and overlong prayers are two extremes, each of which it is equally necessary to avoid.

If it should happen that you are obliged to travel on Sunday or to attend to some unforeseen business, do not be disquieted about the impossibility of fulfilling your customary devout exercises. Replace these with pious aspirations, which, as I have already said, can, in case of necessity, supply for the omission of all other prayers.

Note, in conclusion, that to assist at Mass suffices strictly speaking for the sanctification of the Sunday or holy day. Even this may be omitted by those persons whom duty obliges to attend the sick or to take care of young children; for these being works of justice and charity and good in themselves, may, when performed with a pure intention and accompanied by aspirations, equal and even surpass in value all exterior practices of devotion. I do not speak at all of the sick, for by their sufferings they can sanctify every day and make each one equal to the greatest feast day.

"Worldly notions are forever blending with our thoughts and throwing them out of perspective," St. Francis de Sales says. "In the house of an earthly prince, it is not so honorable to be a scullion in the kitchen as to be a gentleman-in-waiting. But it is different in the house of God, where those in the humblest positions are oft-times the most worthy; for although they labor and drudge, it is done for the love of God and in fulfillment of His divine will. And the true value of our actions is fixed by this divine will and not by their exterior character."

Therefore, he who truly loves God's will in the accomplishment of his duties does not allow his affections to become engaged in any of his spiritual exercises; and so, if sickness or accident interferes with them, he experiences no regret. I do not say indeed that he does not love his devotions, but that he is not attached to them.[68]

If you have a sincere regard for the virtues of obedience and submission, I wish that, should justice or charity demand it, you would forego your pious exercises, which would be a sort of obedience, and that this omission would be supplied by love. I told you on another occasion: the less we live according to our own liking,

[68] Letters to Jane de Chantal, October 14, 1604, and to Madame Brulart, October 1606; cf. *Thy Will Be Done*, 234, 233, 60.

and the less option we have in our actions, the more goodness and solidity will there be in our devotion. It is right and proper sometimes to leave our Lord in order to oblige others for love of Him.

Part Two

꜁

Developing Inner Peace

Chapter Eight

❦

Hope in God's mercy

"Cast all your solicitude upon Him,
for He hath care of you."

1 Peter 5:7

"Let Thy mercy descend upon us according
to the trust we have placed in Thee."

Cant. Saint Ambrose

"Blessed is the man who hopes in the Lord,"[69] says the Holy Spirit. The weakness of our souls is often attributable to lukewarmness in regard to the Christian virtue of hope.

Hold fast to this great truth: he who hopes for nothing will obtain nothing; he who hopes for little will obtain little; he who hopes for all things will obtain all things.

The mercy of God is infinitely greater than all the sins of the world. We should not, then, confine ourselves to a consideration of our own wretchedness, but, rather, we should turn our thoughts to the contemplation of this divine attribute of mercy.

"What do you fear?" says St. Thomas of Villanova.[70] "This Judge whose condemnation you dread is the same Jesus Christ who died upon the Cross in order not to condemn you."

Sorrow, not fear, is the sentiment our sins should awaken in us. When St. Peter said to his divine Master, "Depart from me, O Lord, for I am a sinful man," what did our Savior reply? "Fear not."[71] St. Augustine remarks that, in the Holy Scriptures, we always find hope and love preferred to fear.

[69] Cf. Ps. 145:5 (RSV = Ps. 146:5).
[70] St. Thomas of Villanova (1488-1555), Archbishop of Valencia.
[71] Luke 5:8, 10.

God loves you despite your sins

Our miseries form the throne of the divine mercy, we are told by St. Francis de Sales,[72] for if in the world there were neither sins to pardon, nor sorrows to soothe, nor maladies of the soul to heal, God would not have to exercise the most beautiful attribute of His divine essence. This was our Lord's reason for saying that He came into the world not for the just but for sinners.[73]

Assuredly our faults are displeasing to God, but He does not on their account cease to cherish our souls.

It is unnecessary to observe that this applies only to such faults as are due to the frailty inherent in our nature, and against which an upright will, sustained by divine grace, continually struggles. A perverse will, without which there can be no mortal sin, alienates us from God and renders us hateful in His eyes as long as we are subject to it.

At the feast spoken of in the Gospel, the King receives with love the poor, the blind, and the lame who are clothed with the nuptial garment — that is to say, all those whom a desire to please God maintains in a state of grace, notwithstanding their natural defects and frailty — but His rigorous justice displays itself against him who dares to appear there without this garment.[74] This distinction, found everywhere throughout the Gospels, is essential in order to inspire us with

---

[72] Cf. Letter to Jane Frances de Chantal, August 6, 1606; *Thy Will Be Done*, 142.

[73] Matt. 9:13; Mark 2:17; Luke 5:32.

[74] Cf. Luke 14:16-23; Matt. 22:2-13.

a tender confidence when we fall, without diminishing our horror for deliberate sins.

A good mother is afflicted at the natural defects and infirmities of her child, but she loves him nonetheless, and she does not refuse him her compassion or her aid. Far from it, for the more miserable and suffering and deformed he is, the greater is her tenderness and solicitude for him.

We have, says St. Paul, a good and indulgent High Priest who knows how to have compassion for our weakness: Jesus Christ, who has been pleased to become at once our Brother and our Mediator.[75]

Do not fear what awaits you in eternity

Do not forfeit your peace of mind by wondering what destiny awaits you in eternity. Your future lot is in the hands of God, and it is much safer there than in your own keeping.

The immoderate fear of Hell, in the opinion of St. Francis de Sales, cannot be cured by arguments, but by submission and humility. Hence it was that St. Bernard, when tempted by the Devil to a sin of despair, retorted, "I have not merited Heaven; I know that as well as you do, Satan. But I also know that Jesus Christ, my Savior, has merited it for me. It was not for Himself that He purchased so many merits, but for me. He cedes them to me, and it is by Him and in Him that I shall save my soul."

Far from allowing yourself to be dejected by fear and doubt, raise your desires rather to great virtues and to the most sublime perfection. God loves courageous souls, St. Teresa assures

---

[75] Cf. Heb. 4:15.

us, provided they mistrust their own strength and place all their reliance upon Him. The Devil tries to persuade you that it is pride to have exalted aspirations and to wish to imitate the virtues of the saints, but do not permit him to deceive you by this artifice. He will only laugh at you if he succeeds in making you fall into weakness and irresolution.

To aspire to the noblest and highest ends gives firmness and perseverance to the soul.

⚶

Suggestion for
further reading:

Imitation of Christ, Bk. 3, ch. 30

Chapter Nine

❧

Dwell always in God's presence

"Walk before me, and be perfect."

Genesis 17:1

"I have lifted up my eyes to the mountains
from whence help shall come to me."

Psalm 120:1
(RSV = Psalm 121:1)

❧

The constant remembrance of God's presence is a means of perfection that Almighty God Himself prescribed to the patriarch Abraham. But this practice must be followed gently and without effort or disturbance of mind. The God of love and peace wishes that all we do for Him should be done lovingly and peacefully.

Only in Heaven shall we be able to think actually and uninterruptedly of God. In this world, to do so is an impossibility, for we are at every moment distracted by our occupations, our necessities, and our imagination. We only exhaust ourselves by futile efforts if we try to lead before the proper time an existence similar to that of the angels and saints.

Frequently the fear comes to you that you have failed to keep yourself in the presence of God because you have not thought of Him. This is a mistaken idea. You can, without this definite thought, perform all your actions for love of God and in His presence, by virtue of the intention you had in beginning them.

❧

Act always for God's glory

Now, to act is better than to think. Although the doctor may not have the invalid in mind while he is preparing the medicine that is to restore him to health, nevertheless it is for him he is working, and he is more useful to his patient in this way than if he contented himself with merely thinking of him.

In like manner, when you fulfill your domestic or social duties, when you eat or walk, when you devote yourself to study or to manual labor, even if it is without definitely thinking of God, you are acting for Him, and this ought to suffice to set your mind at rest in regard to the merit of your actions. St. Paul does not say that we must eat, drink, and labor with an actual remembrance of God's presence, but with the habitual intention of glorifying Him and doing His holy will. We fulfill this condition by making an offering to God each morning of all the actions of the day and renewing the act interiorly whenever we can remember to do so.

For this purpose, make frequent use of aspirations. We have already spoken of them. Accustom yourself to make these pious aspirations naturally and without effort, and let them for the most part be expressive of confidence and love.

Should it happen that a considerable space of time elapses without your having thought distinctly of God or raised your heart to Him by any loving aspiration, do not allow this omission to worry you. The servant has performed his duty and deserves well of his master when he has done his will, even though he may not have been thinking of him all the while. Always bear in mind the fact that it is better to work for God than to think of Him. Thought has its highest spiritual value when it results in action; action is meritorious in itself by virtue of the good intention that preceded it.

Chapter Ten

❧

Develop a humble spirit

"If I glorify myself, my glory is nothing."
John 8:54

"For behold, I was born in iniquities,
and in sin did my mother conceive me."
Psalm 50:7
(RSV = Psalm 51:5)

Few persons have a correct idea of the virtue of humility. It is frequently confused with servility or littleness.

To attribute to God what is God's — that is to say, everything that is good — and to ourselves what is ours — that is to say, everything that is evil — these are the essential characteristics of true humility.

Hence, it would appear at first sight that simple good sense ought to suffice to make men humble. Such would be the case were it not that our faculties have been impaired and vitiated in their very source by pride, that direful and ineffaceable consequence of Original Sin. The first man, a creature owing his existence directly to God, was bound to dedicate it entirely to Him and to pay continual homage for it is as for all the other gifts he had received. This was a duty of simple justice. The day whereon he asserted a desire to be independent, he caused an utter derangement in the relations of the creature with his Creator. Pride, that tendency to self-sufficiency, to refer to self the use of the faculties received from God, which was introduced into the soul of the first man by a free act of his will, has attached itself as an indelible stigma to the souls of all his descendants and has become forevermore a part of their nature.

From it comes this inclination, ever springing up afresh, to be independent, to be something of ourselves, to desire for ourselves esteem, affection, and honor, despite the precepts of the divine law, the claims of justice, and the warnings of reason. And thus it is that the whole spiritual life is but one long and painful conflict against this vicious propensity. Divine grace, although sustaining us in the combat, never gives us a complete victory, for the struggle must endure until death — the closing chastisement of our original degradation and the only one that can obliterate the last traces thereof.[76]

As God drew from nothingness everything that exists, in like manner does He wish to lay the foundations of our spiritual perfection upon the knowledge of our nothingness. St. Bonaventure[77] used to say, "Provided God be all, what matters is that I am nothing!"

When a Christian who is truly humble commits a fault, he repents but is not disquieted, because he is not surprised that what is naught but misery, weakness, and corruption should be miserable, weak, and corrupt. He thanks God, on the contrary, that his fall has not been more serious. Thus St. Catherine of Genoa,[78] whenever she found she was guilty of some imperfection, would calmly exclaim, "Another weed from my garden!" This peaceful contemplation of our sinfulness was considered very important by St. Francis de Sales also, for he says, "Let us learn to bear with our imperfections if we wish to attain perfection, for this practice nourishes the virtue of humility."[79]

---

[76] Cf. *Imitation of Christ*, Bk. 3, chs. 13-22.

[77] St. Bonaventure (c. 1217-1274), Franciscan theologian.

[78] St. Catherine of Genoa (1447-1510), mystic.

[79] Letter to Mademoiselle de Soulfour, July 22, 1603; cf. *Thy Will Be Done*, 170.

Humility recognizes God's gifts

Some persons have the erroneous idea that, in order to be humble, they must not recognize in themselves any virtue or talent whatsoever. The reverse is the case according to St. Thomas, for he says it is necessary to realize the gifts we have received, so that we may return thanks for them to Him from whom we hold them. To ignore them is to fail in gratitude toward God and to neglect the object for which He gave them to us. All that we have to do is avoid the folly of taking glory to ourselves because of them. Mules, asses, and donkeys may be laden with gold and perfumes and yet be nonetheless dull and stupid animals.[80] The graces we have received, far from giving us any personal claims, only serve to increase our debt to Him who is their source and their donor.

Praise is naturally more pleasing to us than censure. There is nothing sinful in this preference, for it springs from an instinct of our human nature of which we cannot entirely divest ourselves. But the praise must be always referred to God, for they are His gifts that are praised in us; we are but their bearers and custodians and shall one day have to render Him an account for them in accordance with their value.

The soul that is most humble will also have the greatest courage and the most generous confidence in God; the more it distrusts itself, the more it will trust in Him on whom it relies for all its strength, saying with St. Paul, "I can do all things in Him who strengtheneth me."[81] St. Thomas clearly proves that

---

[80] *Introduction to the Devout Life*, Part 3, ch. 5.
[81] Phil. 4:13.

true Christian humility, far from debasing the soul, is the principle of everything that is really noble and generous. He who refuses the work to which God calls him because of the honor and éclat that accompany it is not humble, but mistrustful and pusillanimous. We shall find in obedience light to show us with certainty that to which we are called and to preserve us from the illusions of self-love and of our natural inclinations.

"We should be actuated by a generous and noble humility," says St. Francis de Sales, "a humility that does nothing in order to be praised and omits nothing that ought to be done through fear of being praised."

It is even good and sometimes necessary to make known the gifts we have received from God and the good works of which divine grace has made us the instruments, when this manifestation can conduce to the glory of God's name, the welfare of the Church, or the edification of the faithful. It was for this threefold object that St. Paul spoke of his apostolic labors and supernatural revelations.

Chapter Eleven

⇛

Abandon yourself to God's will

"Yea, Father, because so it has pleased Thee."
Luke 10:21

"O my Father, if it be possible,
let this chalice pass from me
Nevertheless not as I will, but as Thou wilt."
Matthew 26:39

꩜

We should recognize and adore the will of God in everything that happens to us. The malice of men, or of the Devil himself, can cause nothing to befall us except what is permitted by God. Our divine Lord has declared that not a hair of our heads can fall unless by the will of our heavenly Father.[82]

Therefore, in every condition painful to nature, whether you are afflicted by sickness, assailed by temptations, or tortured by the injustice of men, consider the divine will, and say to God with a loving and submissive heart, "Thy will be done. O my Savior, do with me what Thou willest, as Thou willest, and when Thou willest."

By this means, we render supportable the severest pain and the most trying circumstances. "Do you not feel the infinite sweetness contained in that one phrase, 'the will of God'?" asks St. Mary Magdalene de' Pazzi.[83] Like the wood shown to Moses that drew from the water all its bitterness,[84] it sweetens whatever is bitter in our lives.

Without this practice, so conformable to faith, and without the light and strength that result from it, the afflictions and

---

[82] Cf. Matt. 10:30.

[83] St. Mary Magdalene de' Pazzi (1566-1607), Carmelite mystic.

[84] Exod. 15:25.

pains of life would become unbearable. This is what St. Philip Neri meant when he said, "It rests with man to place himself, even in this life, either in Heaven or in Hell. He who suffers tribulations with patience enjoys celestial peace in advance; he who does not do so has a foretaste of the torments of Hell."

Spiritual progress comes through
suffering for the love of God

Not only does God send or permit our troubles, but He does so for the good of our souls and for our spiritual progress. Do not, then, make a matter of complaint that which should be a motive for gratitude.

St. Francis de Sales says that the Cross is the royal door to the temple of sanctity, and the only one by which we can enter it. One moment spent upon the Cross is therefore more conducive to our spiritual advancement than the anticipated enjoyment of all the delights of Heaven. The happiness of those who have reached their destination consists in the possession of God; to suffer for the love of Him is the only true happiness that those still on the way can expect to attain. Our Lord declared that those who mourn during this exile are blessed, for they shall be consoled eternally in their celestial fatherland.[85]

You are not expected to love suffering

Notice that I say *to suffer for the love of God*, for, as St. Augustine remarks, no person can love suffering in itself. That is

---

[85] Cf. Matt. 5:4.

contrary to nature, and moreover, there would no longer be any suffering if we could accept it with natural relish. But a resigned soul loves to suffer — that is, it loves the virtue of patience and ardently desires the merits that result from the practice of it. A calm and submissive longing to be delivered from our cross if such be the will of God is not inconsistent with the most perfect resignation. This desire is a natural instinct that supernatural grace regulates, moderates, and teaches us to control, but which it never entirely destroys. Our divine Savior Himself, to show that He was truly man, was pleased to feel it as we do, and prayed that the chalice of His Passion might be spared Him.

Hence, you are not required to be stolidly indifferent or to arm yourself with the stern insensibility of the Stoics; that would not be resignation, or humility, or any virtue whatsoever. The essential thing is to suffer with Christian patience and generous resignation everything that is naturally displeasing to us. This is what both reason and Faith prescribe.

Follow Christ's example of resignation

The Redeemer of the world seems to wish to show us in His agony the degree of perfection that the weakness of human nature can attain amid the anguish of sorrow. In the inferior portion of the soul, where the faculty of feeling resides, we find instinctive repugnance to suffering, humble prayer for relief if it please God to accord it; and in the superior portion of the soul, where the will resides, entire resignation if this consolation be denied. A desire for more than this, unless we are called to it by a special grace, would be foolish pride, as we should thus attempt to change the conditions of our nature, whereas our duty is to accept them in order to combat them and to suffer in so doing.[86]

In the following terms, St. Francis de Sales proposes to us this same example of our Savior's resignation during His agony: "Consider the great dereliction our divine Master suffered in the Garden of Olives. See how this beloved Son, having asked for consolation from His loving Father and knowing that it was not His will to grant it, thinks no more about it, no longer craves or looks for it, but, as though He had never sought it, valiantly and courageously completes the work of our redemption. Let it be the same with you. If your heavenly Father sees fit to deny you the consolation you have prayed for, dismiss it from your mind and animate your courage to fulfill your work upon the Cross as if you were never to descend from it nor should ever again see the atmosphere of your life pure and serene."

The same saint also gives us some sublime lessons in resignation applied to the trials and temptations that beset the spiritual life. He draws them from this great and simple thought that serves as foundation for the *Spiritual Exercises* of St. Ignatius — namely, that salvation being the sole object of our existence, and all the attendant circumstances of life only means for attaining it, nothing has any absolute value; and that the only way of forming a true estimate of things is to consider in how far they are calculated to advance or retard the end in view. Accordingly, what difference does it make if we attain this end by riches or poverty, by health or sickness, by

---

[86] Cf. *Imitation of Christ*, Bk. 3, chs. 18, 19.

spiritual consolation or aridity, or by the esteem or contempt of our fellowmen?

So say faith and reason, but human nature revolts against this indifference, as it is well it should; otherwise, how could we acquire merit? Hence, there is a conflict on this point between the flesh and the spirit, and it is this conflict that for a Christian is called life.

Would to God that we did not concern ourselves so much about the road whereon we journey, but rather would keep our eyes fixed on our Guide and upon that blessed country whither He is conducting us. What should it matter to us if it be through deserts or pleasant fields that we walk, provided God be with us and we be advancing toward Heaven? . . .

In short, for the honor of God, acquiesce perfectly in His divine will, and do not suppose that you can serve Him better in any other way; for no one ever serves Him well who does not serve Him as He wishes. Now, He wishes that you serve Him without relish, without feeling, nay, with repugnance and perturbation of spirit. This service does not afford you any satisfaction, it is true, but it pleases Him; it is not to your taste, but it is to His. . . .

Mortify yourself, then, cheerfully, and in proportion as you are prevented from doing the good you desire, do all the more ardently that which you do not desire. You do not wish to be resigned in this case, but you will be so in some other: resignation in the first instance will be of much greater value to you. . . . In fine, let us be what

God wishes, since we are entirely devoted to Him, and would not wish to be anything contrary to His will; for if we were the most exalted creatures under Heaven, of what use would it be to us, if we were not in accord with the will of God? . . .

You should resign yourself perfectly into the hands of God. When you have done your best toward carrying out your design, He will be pleased to accept everything you do, even though it be something less good. You cannot please God better than by sacrificing to Him your will, and remaining in tranquillity, humility, and devotion, entirely reconciled and submissive to His divine will and good pleasure. You will be able to recognize these plainly enough when you find that, notwithstanding all your efforts, it is impossible for you to gratify your wishes.

For God in His infinite goodness sometimes sees fit to test our courage and love by depriving us of the things which it seems to us would be advantageous to our souls; and if He finds us very earnest in their pursuit, yet humble, tranquil, and resigned to do without them if He wishes us to, He will give us more blessings than we would have had in the possession of what we craved. God loves those who at all times and in all circumstances can say to Him simply and heartily, "Thy will be done."[87]

---

[87] St. Francis de Sales, Letters to Jane de Chantal, February 18, 1605, to Madame Brulart, October 1606 and June 10, 1605, and to Mademoiselle Clément, October 1608; cf. *Thy Will Be Done*, 206, 207, 62, 20, 3-4.

Chapter Twelve

Maintain interior peace

"Martha, Martha, thou art careful,
and art troubled about many things."
Luke 10:41

"Always active, always at rest."
St. Augustine

Be on your guard lest your zeal degenerate into anxiety and eagerness. St. Francis de Sales was a most pronounced enemy of these two defects. They cause us to lose sight of God in our actions and make us very prone to impatience if the slightest obstacle should interfere with our designs. It is only by acting peacefully that we can serve the God of peace in an acceptable manner.

"Let us not suffer our peace to be disturbed by precipitousness in our exterior actions. When our bodies or minds are engaged in any work, we should perform it peacefully and with composure, not prescribing for ourselves a definite time to finish it, nor being too anxious to see it completed."[88]

Act without anxiety or agitation

Martha was engaged in a good work when she prepared a repast for our divine Lord; nevertheless He reproved her because she performed it with anxiety and agitation. This goes to show, says St. Francis de Sales, that it is not enough to do good; the good must, moreover, be done well — that is to say,

---

[88] Lorenzo Scupoli, *Treatise on Peace of Soul and Interior Happiness*, ch. 2.

with love and tranquillity. If one turns the spinning wheel too rapidly, it falls and the thread breaks.

Whenever we are doing well, we are always doing enough and doing it sufficiently fast. Those persons who are restless and impetuous do not accomplish any more and what they do is done badly.

St. Francis de Sales was never seen in a hurry, no matter how varied or numerous might be the demands made upon his time. When, on a certain occasion, some surprise was expressed at this, he said, "You ask me how it is that, although others are agitated and flurried, I am not likewise uneasy and in haste. What would you? I was not put in this world to cause fresh disturbance. Is there not enough of it already without my adding to it by my excitability?"

However, do not, on the other hand, succumb to sloth and indifference. All extremes are to be avoided. Cultivate a tranquil activity and an active tranquillity.

In order to acquire tranquillity in action, it is necessary to consider carefully what we are capable of accomplishing and never to undertake more than that. It is self-love, ever more anxious to do much than to do well, which urges us on to burden ourselves with great undertakings and to impose upon ourselves numerous obligations. It maintains and nourishes itself on this tension of mind, this restless anxiety which it takes for infallible signs of a superior capacity. Thus St. Francis de Sales was wont to say, "Our self-love is a great braggart that wishes to undertake everything and accomplishes nothing."

It appears to me that you are overeager and anxious in the pursuit of perfection. . . . Now, I tell you truthfully, as it is said in the book of Kings, that God is not in the great and strong wind, nor in the earthquake, nor in the fire, but in the gentle movement of an almost imperceptible breeze.[89] ... Anxiety and agitation contribute nothing toward success. The desire of success is good, but only if it is not accompanied by solicitude.

I expressly forbid you to give way to disquietude, for it is the mother of all imperfections. ... Peace is necessary in all things and everywhere. If any trouble comes to us, either of an interior or exterior nature, we should receive it peacefully. If joy be ours, it should be received peacefully. If we have to flee from evil, we should do it peacefully; otherwise we may fall in our flight and thus give our enemy a chance to kill us. Is there a good work to be done? We must do it peacefully, or else we shall commit many faults by our hastiness. And even as regards penance, that, too, must be done peacefully. "Behold," said the prophet, "in peace is my bitterness most bitter."

---

[89] 3 Kings 19:11-13 (RSV = 1 Kings 19:11-13).

Chapter Thirteen

༉

Yield not to sadness

"I rejoiced at the things that were said to me:
we shall go into the house of the Lord. . . .
Sing joyfully to God, all the earth:
serve ye the Lord with gladness. . . .
Why art thou sad, O my soul, and
why dost thou trouble me?"

Psalms 121:1, 99:1, 42:5
(RSV = Psalms 122:1, 100:1-2, 43:5)

"And God shall wipe away
all tears from their eyes."

Apocalypse 21:4
(RSV = Revelation 21:4)

‭❧

Sadness, says St. Francis de Sales, is the worst thing in the world, sin alone excepted. It is a dangerous error to seek recollection in sadness. It is the spirit of God that produces recollection; sadness is the work of the spirit of darkness.

Do not forget the rule given by St. Francis de Sales for the discernment of spirits: any thought that troubles and disquiets us cannot come from the God of peace, who makes His dwelling place only in peaceful souls. "Always be as happy as you can in well-doing," he says, "for it gives a double value to good works to be well done and to be done cheerfully. And when I say rejoice in well-doing, I do not mean that if you happen to commit some fault, you should on that account abandon yourself to sadness. For the sake of God, no; for that would be to add defect to defect. But I mean that you should persevere in the wish to do well, that you return to it the moment you realize you have deviated from it, and that by means of this fidelity, you live happily in the Lord."

"May God be ever in our heart," says St. Francis de Sales. "Live joyfully and be generous, for this is the will of God, whom we love and to whose service we are consecrated."[90]

---

[90] St. Francis de Sales, Letter to Jane de Chantal, August 28, 1605; cf. *Thy Will Be Done*, 214; *Imitation of Christ*, Bk. 3, ch. 47.

❧

Diversions ward off sadness

It is wrong to deny oneself all diversion. The mind becomes fatigued and depressed by remaining always concentrated in itself and thus more easily falls a prey to sadness. St. Thomas says explicitly that one may incur sin by refusing all innocent amusement. Every excess, no matter what its nature, is contrary to order and consequently to virtue.

Recreations and amusements are to the life of the soul what seasoning is to our corporal food. Food that is too highly seasoned quickly becomes injurious and sometimes fatal in its effects; that which is not seasoned at all soon becomes unendurable because of its insipidity and unpalatableness.

As to the amount of diversion it is right to take, no absolute measure can be given; the rule is that each person should have as much as is necessary for him. This quantity varies according to the bent of the mind, the nature of the habitual occupations, and the greater or lesser predisposition to sadness one observes in his disposition.

When you find your heart growing sad, divert yourself without a moment's delay; make a visit, enter into conversation with those around you, read some amusing book, take a walk, sing — do something; it matters not what, provided you close the door of your heart against this terrible enemy. As the sound of a trumpet gives the signal for a combat, so sad thoughts apprise the Devil that a favorable moment has come for him to attack us.

Chapter Fourteen

Have a spirit of liberty

"Now, the Lord is a spirit,
and where the spirit of Lord is,
there is liberty."

2 Corinthians 3:17

"For you have not received the
spirit of bondage again in fear; but you
have received the spirit of adoption of sons,
whereby we cry, 'Abba, Father.' "

Romans 8:15

"Love God and do what you will."

St. Augustine

Christian liberty of spirit, so earnestly recommended by the saints, consists in not becoming the slave of anything, even if good, unless it be of God's will. Thus, our purest inclinations, our holiest habits, and our wisest rules of conduct should yield without murmur or complaint to every manifest of this divine will, in order that they never become for us obstacles or impediments to good or the occasion of trouble and disquietude. By this means only can we perform all our actions with cheerful confidence and devout courage.

"I leave you the spirit of liberty — not that liberty which hinders obedience, for such is the liberty of the flesh, but that which excludes scruples and constraint. . . . We ask of God above all things that His name be hallowed, that His kingdom come, that His will be done on earth as it is in Heaven. All this implies the spirit of liberty; for provided God's name be sanctified, that His divine Majesty reign in you, and that His will be done, the spirit desires nothing more."[91]

St. Francis de Sales says, "He who possesses the spirit of liberty will on no account allow his affections to be mastered even by his spiritual exercises, and in this way, he avoids

---

[91] St. Francis de Sales, Letter to Jane de Chantal, October 14, 1604; cf. *Thy Will Be Done,* 233-234.

feeling any regret if they are interfered with by sickness or accident. I do not say that he does not love his devotions, but that he is not attached to them."[92]

A soul that is attached to meditation, if interrupted, will show chagrin and impatience; a soul that has true liberty will take the interruption in good part and show a gracious countenance to the person who was the cause of it. For it is all one to it whether it serves God by meditating or by bearing with its neighbor. Both duties are God's will, but, just at this time, patience with others is the more essential.

Liberty of spirit guides your actions

The fruits of this holy liberty of spirit are prompt and tranquil submission and generous confidence. St. Francis de Sales relates that St. Ignatius ate meat one day in Holy Week simply because his physician thought it expedient for him to do so on account of a slight illness. A spirit of constraint would have made him allow the doctor to spend three days in persuading him, he adds, and he would then very probably have refused to yield. I cite this example for the benefit of timid souls and not for those who seek to elude an obligation by unwarranted dispensations.

This matter is of such importance and a just medium so difficult to follow in practice, that it seems useful to transcribe the following passage from St. Francis de Sales in its entirety, with the rules and examples it contains, in order that the

---

[92] Letter to Jane de Chantal, October 14, 1604; cf. *Thy Will Be Done*, 234.

proper occasions for the exercise of this virtue and its limitations may be well understood:

> A heart possessed of this spirit of liberty is not attached to consolations, but receives afflictions with all the sweetness that is possible to human nature. I do not say that it does not love and desire consolations, but that its affections are not wedded to them. . . . It seldom loses its joy, for no privation saddens a heart that is not set upon any one thing. I do not say it never loses it, but if it does so, it quickly regains it. The effects of this virtue are sweetness of temper, gentleness, and forbearance toward everything that is not sin or occasion of sin forming a disposition gently susceptible to the influences of charity and of every other virtue.

The occasions for exercising this holy freedom are found in all those things that happen contrary to our natural inclinations; for one whose affections are not engaged in his own will does not lose patience when his desires are thwarted.

There are two vices opposed to this liberty of spirit: instability and constraint, or dissipation and servility. The former is a certain excess of freedom that causes us to change our devout exercises or state of life without reason and without knowing if it be God's will. On the slightest pretext, practices, plans, and rules are altered, and for every trivial obstacle, our laudable customs are abandoned. In this way, the heart is dissipated and spent and becomes like an orchard open on all sides, the fruit whereof is not for the owner but for the passersby. Constraint, or servility, is a certain lack of liberty owing to which the mind is overwhelmed with vexation or anger when we cannot carry out our designs, even though we might be doing something better.

For example, I resolve to make a meditation every morning. Now, if I have the spirit of instability, or dissipation, I am apt to defer it until evening for the most insignificant reason, because I was kept awake by the barking of a dog, or because I have a letter to write, even if it is not at all pressing. If, on the contrary, I have the spirit of constraint, or servility, I will not give up my meditation even if a sick person has great need of my aid just then, or if I have an important and urgent dispatch to send which should not be deferred, and so on.

It remains for me to give you some examples of true liberty of spirit which will make you understand it better than I can explain it. But, before doing so . . . I should say there are two rules which it is necessary to observe in order not to make any mistake on the subject.

The first is that a person must never abandon his pious practices and the common rules of virtue unless it is plainly evident that God wills that he do so. Now, this will is manifested in two ways: through necessity and through charity. I desire to preach this Lent in some little corner of my diocese; however, if I get sick or break my leg, I need not give way to regret or disquietude because I cannot do as I intended, for it is evident that it is the will of God that I serve Him by suffering and not by preaching. Or, even if I am not ill or crippled, but an occasion presents itself of going to some other place which, if I do not avail myself of, the people there may become Huguenots, the will of God is sufficiently manifest to make me amiably change my plans.

The second rule is that when it is necessary to make use of this liberty of spirit from motives of charity, care should be taken that it is done without scandal or injustice. For instance, I may know that I should be more useful in some distant place not within my own diocese. I would have no freedom of choice in this matter, for my obligations are here and I would give scandal and do an injustice by abandoning my charge.

Thus, it is a false idea of the spirit of liberty that would induce married women to keep aloof from their husbands without legitimate reason, under pretext of devotion and charity. . . . This spirit rightly understood never interferes with the duties of one's vocation nor prejudices them in any way. On the contrary, it makes everyone contented in his state of life, as each should know it is God's will that he remain in it.

St. Charles Borromeo[93] was one of the most austere, exact, and determined of men; bread was his only food, water his only drink. He was so strict that, during the twenty-four years he was an archbishop, he went into his garden but twice and visited his brothers on only two occasions and then because they were ill. Yet this austere priest, when dining with his Swiss neighbors, which he often did in order to move them to amend their lives, did not hesitate to join them in drinking

---

[93] St. Charles Borromeo (1538-1584), Archbishop of Milan.

toasts and healths on every occasion and, in doing so, to take more than was necessary to quench his thirst. Here is true liberty of spirit exemplified in the most mortified man of his time. An unstable spirit would have gone too far; a spirit of constraint would have thought it was committing a mortal sin; a spirit of liberty would act in this way from a motive of charity.

St. Spiridion,[94] a bishop of olden times, once gave shelter to a pilgrim who was almost dying of hunger. It was the season of Lent and in a place where nothing was to be had but salt meat. Spiridion ordered this meat to be cooked, and then gave it to the pilgrim. Seeing that the latter, notwithstanding his great need, hesitated to eat it, the saint, although he did not require it, ate some first in order to remove the poor man's scruples. That was a true spirit of liberty born of charity.[95]

❧

Liberty of spirit dispels fear

Again, it is this Christian spirit of freedom that excludes fear and uneasiness in regard to all those things which God has not permitted us to know. It gives us a sweet and tender confidence as to the pardon of our past sins, the present condition of our souls, and our eternal destiny. It reminds us continually that although we have deserved Hell, our divine Lord has merited Heaven for us, and that it would be doing a great injury to

---

[94] St. Spiridion (died c. 348), Bishop of Tremithus in Cyprus.

[95] Letter to Jane de Chantal, October 14, 1604; cf. *Thy Will Be Done*, 234-237.

His goodness not to hope for pardon for the past, assistance of divine grace for the present, and salvation after death. Finally, it teaches us to drown our remorse for sin in the ocean of the divine mercy.

Do not make rash vows

I earnestly exhort you never to make rash vows in the hope of thus increasing the merit of your ordinary works. One can attain the same end by many ways that are easier and less dangerous. Those who are guilty of this imprudence often run the risk of breaking their vows and of thus sinning gravely. And if they avoid this misfortune, it is only at the expense of their peace of soul, sacrificed to a craven and unquiet servitude that is totally incompatible with the tranquillity and confidence required in the great work of our spiritual perfection.

Many pious persons are too prone to advise obligations of this kind. If they do so to you, humbly excuse yourself by saying that you do not possess the extraordinary virtue requisite in order to fulfill them without disquietude. St. Francis de Sales disapproved of all the particular vows made by St. Jane Frances de Chantal and declared them null. I have almost invariably found persons bound by such solemn obligations restless and agitated, and have frequently seen them exposed to the gravest falls.

Do not allow yourself to be misled by the example of some of the saints who made vows. Rarely is the desire to imitate certain extraordinary practices of theirs an inspiration of divine grace; rather, is it a temptation from the Devil inciting us to pride and temerity. St. Francis de Sales exclaimed, "Give me the spirit that animated St. Bernard, and I shall do what St. Bernard did." Let us apply ourselves, I repeat, to the imitation of those simple and solid virtues by which the saints attained sanctity, and be content to admire those supernatural acts that suppose it already acquired.

To bind oneself by arbitrary vows without compromising salvation, three things are necessary: supernatural inspiration, urging one to make them; extraordinary virtue, so as never to violate them; and unalterable tranquillity, in order to preserve peace of soul in keeping them.

⚓

Suggestion for
further reading:

Imitation of Christ, Bk. 3, ch. 26

Chapter Fifteen

⁂

Strive for Christian perfection

"Conduct me, O Lord, in Thy way,
and I will walk in Thy truth."

Psalm 85:11
(RSV = Psalm 86:11)

"Except the Lord build the house,
they labor in vain who build it."

Psalm 126:1
(RSV = Psalm 127:1)

A Christian is not obliged to be perfect, but to tend continually toward perfection; that is to say, he must labor unceasingly and with all his strength to increase in virtue. To make no attempt to advance is to go back.

You see, it is a question not of succeeding but of laboring earnestly and sincerely. Success does not depend upon us. God grants that or refuses it or defers it according to what He knows is best for us.

"Let us do three things," says St. Francis de Sales. "First, have a pure intention to look in all things to the honor and glory of God; second, do the little we can toward this end, according to the advice of our spiritual father; third, leave the care of all the rest to God. Why should he torment himself who has God for the object of his intentions and does all that he can? Why should he be anxious? What has he to fear? God is not terrible for those whom He loves; He is satisfied with little, for He knows well that we have not much to give."[96]

Allow yourself to be governed by God. Do not think so much of yourself. . . . Make a general and universal

---

[96] Letter to the abbess of Puits d'Orbe, April 1605; cf. *Letters to Persons in Religion*, 60.

resolution to serve God in the best manner you are able and do not waste time in examining and sifting so minutely to find out what that may be. This is simply an impertinence due to the condition of your acute and precise mind, which wishes to tyrannize over your will and to control it by fraud and subtlety.

You know that, in general, God wishes that we serve Him by loving Him above all things, and our neighbor as ourselves for love of Him, and in particular, that we fulfill the duties of our state of life; that is all. But it must be done in good faith, without deceit or subterfuge, and in the ordinary way of this world, which is not the home of perfection; humanly, too, and according to the limitations of time; and in a divine and angelic manner and according to eternity being reserved for a future life. . . .

Do not therefore be so anxious to know whether or not you have attained perfection. This should never be; for were we the most perfect creatures on earth, we ought not to dwell upon or glory in it, but always consider ourselves imperfect. Our self-examination must never be for the purpose of discovering if we are imperfect, for this we should never doubt. Hence, it follows that we must not be surprised at seeing ourselves imperfect, since we can never be otherwise in this life; nor on that account give way to despondency, for there is no remedy for it.

But, yes, we can correct our faults gently and gradually, for that is the reason they are left in us. We shall be inexcusable if we do not try to amend them, but quite excusable if we are not entirely successful in doing so, for it is not the same with imperfections as with sins.[97]

Perform your religious
exercises with love

Now, the means to be employed in laboring for perfection and in making progress in virtue do not consist in multiplying prayers, fasts, and other religious practices. Some good religious who had fasted three times a week during an entire year thought that in order to satisfy the obligation of advancing more and more in virtue, they ought to fast four times a week the following year. They consulted St. Francis de Sales on the subject. He laughingly answered them, "If you fast four times a week this year so as to advance in perfection, you will be obliged for the same reason to fast five times the next year, then six, then seven times; and the number of your fasts being always the gauge of the degree of perfection you shall have attained, it will be necessary for you, under pain of advancing no more, thereafter to fast twice a day, then thrice, then four times, and so on." What St. Francis de Sales said of fasting is just as applicable to all other devout practices.

Instead, then, of continually adding to your religious exercises, study to perfect yourself in the practice of those you already perform, doing them with more love and peace of soul, and with greater purity of intention. Should it happen that you are unable to perform all your usual devotions conveniently,

---

[97] St. Francis de Sales, Letter to a novice sister, January 16, 1603; cf. *Letters to Person in Religion*, 22-23.

omit a portion of them so that the remainder may be done with greater tranquillity.

The spirit of perfection, says St. Bernard, does not consist in doing great things, but in doing common and ordinary things perfectly.

Most people, when they wish to reform, pay much more attention to filling their life with certain difficult and extraordinary actions than to purifying their intention and opposing their natural inclinations in the ordinary duties of their state. In this, they often deceive themselves, for it would be much better to make less change in the actions and more in the dispositions of the soul that prompt them. When one is already leading a virtuous and well-regulated life, it is of far greater consequence, in order to become truly spiritual, to change the interior than the exterior. God is not satisfied with the motions of the lips, the posture of the body, or with external ceremonies; what He demands is a will no longer divided between Him and any creature, a will perfectly docile . . . that wishes unreservedly whatever He wishes and never under any pretext wishes anything that He does not wish.

This will, perfectly simple and entirely devoted to God, you should bear with you into all the circumstances of your life, and everywhere that divine Providence leads you. . . . Even mere amusements may be transformed into good works, if you enter into them only through a kindly motive and to conform to the order of God. Happy indeed the heart of her for whom

God opens this way of holy simplicity! She walks therein like a little child holding his mother's hand and allowing her to lead him without any concern as to where he is going. Content to be free, she is ready to speak or to be silent; when she cannot say edifying things, she says commonplace things with an equally good grace. She amuses herself by making what St. Francis de Sales calls *joyeusetés,* playful little jests, with which she diverts others as well as herself.

You will tell me, perhaps, that you would prefer to be occupied with something more serious and solid. But God would not prefer it for you, seeing that He chooses what you would not choose, and you know His taste is better than yours. You would find more consolation in solid things for which He has given you a relish, and it is this consolation of which He wishes to deprive you; it is this relish which He wishes to mortify in you, although it may be good and salutary. The very virtues, as they are practiced by us, need to be purified by the contradictions that God makes them suffer in order to detach them the better from all self-will.

When piety is founded on the fundamental principle of God's holy will, without consulting our own taste, or temperament, or the sallies of an excessive zeal, oh, how simple, sweet, amiable, discreet, and reliable it is in all its movements! A pious person lives much as others do, quite unaffectedly and without apparent austerity, in a sociable and genial way; but with a constant subjection to every duty, an unrelenting renunciation of everything that does not enter into God's designs in her regard, and, finally, with a clear view of God to whom she sacrifices all the irregular inclinations of nature. This, indeed, is the adoration in spirit and in truth desired by Jesus Christ, our Lord, and His eternal Father. Without it, all the rest is but a religion of ceremonial, and rather the shadow than the reality of Christianity.[98]

Follow your own God-given path to holiness

Apply yourself in a particular manner to become perfect in the fulfillment of the duties of your state of life, for, on this, all perfection and sanctity are grounded. When God created the world, He commanded the plants to produce fruit, but each one according to its kind.[99] In like manner, our souls are all obliged to produce fruits of holiness, but each according to its kind — that is to say, according to the position in which God has placed us. Elijah in the desert and David on the throne did not have to become holy by a similar process; and Joshua amid the tumult of arms would have sought in vain to sanctify himself by the same means as Samuel in the peaceful retreat of the Temple.

This instruction is addressed to those who, being placed in the world, would wish to practice there the virtues of the cloister, or, while residing in palaces, would attempt to lead the life of the solitaries of the desert. They bear fruits that are excellent in themselves, no doubt, but not according to their kind, and hence, they do not fulfill the will of God.

[98] François Fénelon, *Christian Perfection*, ch. 2.
[99] Gen. 1:11.

Perfection has but one aim, and it is the same for all — to wit, the love of God — but there are diverse ways of attaining it. Among the saints themselves, we find most striking differences. St. Benedict was never seen to laugh, whereas St. Francis de Sales laughed frequently and was always animated, bright, and cheerful. St. Hilarion[100] considered it an act of sensuality to change his habit, while, on the other hand, St. Catherine of Siena was extremely particular about bodily cleanliness, which she looked upon as a symbol of purity of soul. If you consult St. Jerome, you hear only of fear of the terrible judgments of God; read St. Augustine, and you will find only the language of confidence and love.

The minds, dispositions, and characters of men are as varied as their physiognomies; grace perfects them little by little, but does not change their nature. Hence in our endeavors to imitate the ways of such-and-such a saint for whom we feel a particular attraction, we should not condemn those of the others, but say with the psalmist, "Let every spirit praise the Lord."[101] Consult your director as to whom and what may be most suitable for your imitation.

Do not be discouraged by falls

Never be afraid that you are not following the way of perfection because you still have defects and commit many faults. This was true of the greatest saints, for St. Augustine declares

---

[100] St. Hilarion (c. 291-371), founder of the anchoritic life in Palestine.

[101] Ps. 150:5 (RSV = Ps. 150:6).

that all of them could exclaim with the apostle St. John: "If we claim to be without sin, we deceive ourselves and the truth is not in us."[102] "He who came into the world with sin," says St. Gregory the Great, "cannot live there without sin."

"Act like the little child who, when it feels that his mother is holding him by the sleeve, runs about quite boldly and without being surprised at all the little falls he takes. Thus, as long as you find that God is holding you by the good will and the resolution He has given you to serve Him, go on bravely and do not be astonished that you stumble and fall occasionally. There is no need to be troubled about it, provided that at certain intervals, you cast yourself into your Father's arms and embrace Him with the kiss of charity. Go on your way, then, cheerfully and heartily, doing the best you can; and if it cannot always be cheerfully, let it at least be always courageously and faithfully."[103]

But we must bear in mind the vast difference that exists between the love of sin and sin committed inadvertently or from weakness. Affection for sin is the sole obstacle to perfection. Thus, the most learned Fathers of the Church make a distinction between two kinds of tepidity: that which can be avoided and that which cannot be avoided. The former condition is that of a soul that retains an attachment for certain sins; the other, that of one falling into sin through frailty and from being taken unawares, which has been the case even with the greatest saints.

---

[102] 1 John 1:8.

[103] St. Francis de Sales, Letter to a novice sister, January 16, 1603; cf. *Letters to Persons in Religion*, 24-25.

Therefore, instead of troubling yourself about these accidental falls, inseparable from human nature, make them turn to your spiritual advantage by causing them to increase your humility. It often happens, says St. Gregory the Great, that God allows great defects to remain in some souls at the beginning of their spiritual life so that, by means of them, they may grow in self-knowledge and learn to place their entire confidence in Him. St. Augustine tells us that God, in His infinite wisdom, has been better pleased to bring forth good out of evil than to hinder the evil itself. Thus, when you learn to draw fruits of humility from your faults, you correspond to the sublime designs of God's unspeakable Providence.

Follow true ways of perfection

Should you happen to fear that you are not walking in the true way of perfection, consult your director and place implicit reliance upon the answer he gives you. Who is the saint that has not had to suffer because of a like doubt? But they were all reassured by the consideration of God's infinite goodness and by obedience to their spiritual father.

Some persons, although conscious of a sincere desire to serve God, nevertheless are disposed to feel alarmed about their spiritual condition, at the remembrance of all they have heard and read in regard to false consciences, self-illusion, and the deceptive security of those who are following a wrong path. There are two ways of forming a false conscience: first, by choosing among our duties those for which we feel most attraction and natural tendency, and then, in order to give ourselves up to them more than is necessary, to persuade ourselves we can neglect the others. Thus, a person with a preference for exterior acts of religion will spend all day praying or attending sermons and offices of the Church and considers herself very devout, although she may have been neglecting her temporal duties. Another, being differently disposed, will apply herself exclusively to the duties of her state of life, sacrificing to them without regret those of religion, quite convinced that one who is faithful in all the domestic relations, and gives to everyone his due, cannot possibly be otherwise than pleasing to God.

The second way of making a false conscience consists in giving the preference in our esteem and practice to those among the Christian virtues that find their analogies in our natural dispositions, for there is not one of the virtues that has not its correlative among the various qualities of the human character. Persons of a gentle and placid disposition will affect meekness, the practice of which will be very easy for them and require no effort; and imagining they exercise a Christian virtue when in reality they only follow a natural bent, they are liable to fall into a culpable weakness. Those who, on the contrary, have an exact and rigid mind will esteem justice and order above all else, making small account of meekness and charity; and thus justifying themselves falsely by their natural temperament, they follow the tendency of the flesh while believing they obey the spirit, and may easily become addicted to excessive severity.

It is evident, therefore, that the first rule to be observed in order to avoid these dangerous illusions and to walk securely in the way of perfection is to apply ourselves in a special manner to the practice of those duties for which we feel least innate attraction, and always to mistrust our natural virtues, however good they may appear. Then there is one consideration that should serve to reassure all Christians who are in earnest about their salvation; while they act in good faith and deal frankly and sincerely with their confessor, it is impossible for them to become the victim of a false conscience.

Live according to the spirit

In the following passage, St. Francis de Sales recommends us to watch carefully over our natural tendencies and to substitute for them as much as possible the inspirations of grace, which he calls living according to the spirit:

To live according to the spirit is to think, speak, and act according to the virtues, which are of the spirit, and not according to the senses and feelings, which are of the flesh. These latter we should make serve us, but we must hold them in subjection and not allow them to control us, whereas with the spiritual virtues it is just the reverse; we should serve them and bring everything else under subjection to them. . . . Human nature wishes to have a share in everything that goes on and loves itself so dearly that it considers nothing of any account unless it be mixed up in it. The spirit, on the contrary, attaches itself to God and often says that whatever is not God's is nothing to it; and as through a motive of charity, it takes part in things committed to it, so through humility and self-denial, it willingly gives up all share in those which are denied it. . . . I am diffident and have no self-confidence, and therefore I wish to be allowed to live in a way congenial to this disposition; anyone can see that this is not according to the spirit. . . . But, although I am naturally timorous and retiring, I desire to try to overcome these traits of character and to fulfill all the requirements of the charge imposed upon me by obedience. Who does not see that this is to live according to the spirit?

Hence, as I have said before, to live according to the spirit is to have our actions, our words, and our thoughts such as the Spirit of God would require of us. When I say *thoughts*, I of course mean voluntary thoughts.

I am sad, says someone, consequently I shall not speak; magpies and parrots do the same. I am sad, but as charity requires me to speak, I shall do so; spiritual persons act thus. I am slighted, and I get angry; so do peacocks and monkeys. I am slighted, and I rejoice thereat; that is what the Apostles did.[104]

In short, to live according to the spirit is to do in all circumstances and on all occasions whatever faith, hope, and charity demand of us, without even waiting to consider if we are or are not influenced by our natural disposition.

[104] Letter to a sister of the Visitation; cf. *Letters to Persons in Religion*, 254-256.

Strive for Christian perfection

Achieving perfection takes time

Generally speaking, it is only after a long and painful struggle that one succeeds in climbing the mount of perfection. There are some statues, says St. Francis de Sales, that it has cost the artists thirty years' labor to perfect. Now, the perfecting of a soul is a much more difficult work. We must therefore set about it with tranquillity, patience, and confidence in God. We shall always obtain what we wish soon enough if we obtain it at the time God pleases to grant it.

Suggestion for
further reading:

Imitation of Christ, Bk. 3, ch. 54

Part Three

※

Loving Others

Chapter Sixteen

�֍

Love God and your neighbor

"By this shall all men know
that you are my disciples,
if you have love one for another."

John 13:35

"He who saith he is in the light,
and hateth his brother,
he is in darkness even until now."

1 John 2:9

Our divine Lord has said that His disciples should be known by their love for one another. This Christian virtue of charity makes us love our neighbor in God — the creature for the sake of the Creator. Love of God, love of our neighbor: these virtues are two branches springing from the same trunk and having but one and the same root.

Assist your brethren in their needs whenever you can. However, you should always be careful to consult the laws of prudence in this matter and to be guided by your means and position. By a desire to do good, supply for the material aid you are unable to give.

When your neighbor offends you, he does not cease on that account to be the creature and the image of God; therefore, the Christian motive you have for loving him still exists. He is not, perhaps, worthy of pardon, but has not our Savior Jesus Christ, who so often has forgiven you much more grievous offenses, merited it for him?

Observe, however, that we can scarcely avoid feeling some repugnance for those who have offended us, but to feel and to consent are two distinct and widely different things, as we have already said. When religion commands us to love our enemies, the commandment is addressed to the superior portion of the soul — the will — not to the inferior portion in which reside the carnal affections that follow the natural inclinations. In a word, when we speak of charity, the question is not of that human friendship which we feel for those who are naturally pleasing to us, a sentiment wherein we seek merely our own satisfaction and which therefore has nothing in common with charity.

St. Francis de Sales says this:

> Charity makes us love God above all things, and our neighbor as ourselves with a love not sensual, not natural, not selfish, but pure, strong, and unwavering, and having its foundation in God.
>
> A person is extremely sweet and agreeable, and I love her tenderly; or, she loves me well and does much to oblige me, and on that account I love her in return. Who does not see that this affection is according to the senses and the flesh? For animals that have no soul, but only a body and senses, love those who are good and gentle and kind to them.
>
> Then there is another person who is brusque and uncivil, but, apart from this, is really devout and even desirous of becoming gentler and more courteous; consequently, not for any gratification she affords me, or for any self-interested motive whatever, but solely for the good pleasure of God, I talk to her, aid her, love her. This is the virtue of charity indeed, for nature has no share in it.

The literal and exact fulfillment of the evangelical precept is often found impracticable. How, we say, is it possible to have for all men indiscriminately that extreme sensibility we feel for everything that touches us individually, that constant solicitude for our spiritual or temporal interests, that delicacy of feeling that we reserve for ourselves and for certain objects specially dear to us? And yet our Lord's precept should be observed literally.

What, then, is to be done?

An answer will be found in the following passage from Fénelon, and we shall see that it is not a question of exaggerating the love of one's neighbor, but of moderating self-love, and thus making both the one and the other subordinate to the love of God:

> To love our neighbor as ourselves does not mean that we should have for him that intense feeling of affection that we have for ourselves, but simply that we wish for him, and from the motive of charity, what we wish for ourselves. Pure and genuine love, love having for its sole end the object beloved, should be reserved for God alone, and to bestow it elsewhere is a violation of a divine right.

But although it is forbidden us to show hatred or to entertain it voluntarily against the wicked and those who have offended us, this is not meant to prevent us from defending ourselves or taking such precautions against them as prudence suggests. Christian charity obliges and disposes us to love our enemies and to be good to them when there is occasion to do so, but it should not carry us so far as to protect the wicked, nor leave us without defense against their aggressiveness. It allows us to be vigilant in guarding against their encroachments and to take precautions against their machinations.

How to Love God and Keep His Commandments

*Judge others' actions with
prudence and charity*

Always be ready and willing to excuse the faults of your neighbor, and never put an unfavorable interpretation upon his actions. The same action, says St. Francis de Sales, may be looked upon under many different aspects: a charitable person will ever suppose the best; an uncharitable one will just as certainly choose the worst.

"Do not weigh so carefully the sayings and doings of others, but let your thought of them be simple and good, kindly and affectionate. You should not exact of your neighbor greater perfection than of yourself, nor be surprised at the diversity of imperfections, for an imperfection is not more an imperfection from the fact that it is extravagant and peculiar."

It is very difficult for a good Christian to become really guilty of rash judgment, in the true sense of the word, which is that, without just reasons or sufficient grounds he forms and pronounces in his own mind in a positive manner a condemnation of his neighbor. The grave sin of rash judgment is frequently confounded with suspicion or even simple distrust, which may be justifiable on much slighter grounds.

Suspicion is permissible when it has for its aim measures of just prudence; charity forbids gratuitously malevolent thoughts, but not vigilance and precaution.

Suspicion is not only permissible, but it is at times an important duty for those who are charged with the direction and guardianship of others. Thus, it is a positive obligation for a father in regard to his children, and for a master in regard to his servants, whenever there is occasion to correct some vice they know exists, or to prevent some fault they have reasonable cause to fear.

As to simple mistrust, which should not be confused with suspicion, it is only an involuntary and purely passive condition, to which we may be more or less inclined by our natural disposition without our free will being at all involved. Mistrust, suspicion, and rash judgment are, then, three distinct and very different things, and we should be careful not to confound them.

Chapter Seventeen

❧

Let prudence guide your zeal

"But if you have bitter zeal,
and there be contentions in your heart, glory not,
and be not liars against the truth: for this is not wisdom
descending from above, but earthly, sensual, diabolical."

James 3:14-15

"For the anger of man worketh not the justice of God."

James 1:20

Zeal for the salvation of souls is a sublime virtue, and yet how many errors and sins are every day committed in its name! Evil is never done more effectually and with greater security, says St. Francis de Sales, than when one does it believing he is working for the glory of God. The saints themselves can be mistaken in this delicate matter. We see a proof of this in the incident related of the apostles St. James and St. John, for our Lord reprimanded them for asking Him to cause fire from Heaven to fall upon the Samaritans.[105]

Acts of zeal are like coins, the stamp upon which it is necessary to examine attentively, as there are more counterfeits than good ones. To be pure, zeal should be accompanied with very great humility, for it is of all virtues the one into which self-love most easily glides. When it does so, zeal is apt to become imprudent, presumptuous, unjust, and bitter. Let us consider these characteristics in detail.

Zeal calls for reflection and prudence

In every soil, there grows some thorn — something, in other words, that needs correction, for the best soil is seldom

---

[105] Luke 9:54.

without its noxious weed. Imprudent zeal, by seeking awkwardly to pluck out the thorn, often succeeds only in plunging it farther in, thus rendering the wound deeper and more painful. In such a case, it is essential to act with reflection and great prudence. There is a time to speak and a time to be silent, says the Holy Spirit.[106] Prudent zeal is silent when it realizes that to be so is less hurtful than to speak.

Zeal must not be meddlesome

Some persons are even presumptuous enough in their mistaken zeal to meddle in the domestic affairs of other families, blaming, counseling, attempting to reform without measure or discretion, and thus causing an evil much greater than the one they wish to correct. Let us employ the activity of our zeal in our own reformation, says St. Bernard, and pray humbly for that of others. It is great presumption on our part thus to assume the role of apostles when we are not as yet even good and faithful disciples. Not that you should by any means be indifferent to the salvation of souls; on the contrary, you must wish it most ardently, but do not undertake to effect it except with great prudence, humility, and diffidence in self.

Zeal respects diversity

Again, there are pious persons whose zeal consists in wishing to make everybody adopt their particular practices of devotion. Such a one, if he has a special attraction for meditating

[106] Eccles. 3:7.

on the Passion of our divine Lord or for visiting the Blessed Sacrament, would like to oblige everyone, under pain of reprobation, to pass long hours prostrate before the crucifix or the tabernacle. Another who is especially devoted to visiting the poor and the sick and to the other works of corporal mercy, acknowledges no piety apart from these excellent practices.

Now, this is not an enlightened zeal. Martha and Mary were sisters, says St. Augustine, but they have not a like office: one acts, the other contemplates. If both had passed the day in contemplation, no one would have prepared a repast for their divine Master; if both had been employed in this material work, there would have been no one to listen to His words and garner up His divine lessons. The same thing may be said of other good works. In choosing among them, each person should follow the inspirations of God's grace, and these are quite varied. The eye that sees but hears not must neither envy nor blame the ear that hears but sees not. "Let every spirit praise the Lord," says the royal prophet.[107]

St. Paul condemned in strong terms those Christians who showed too exclusive a preference for their spiritual masters — some admitting as truth only what came from the mouth of Peter, others acknowledging none save Paul, and others again none but Apollo. "What?" said he to them, "Is not Jesus Christ the same for all of you? Is it, then, Paul who was crucified for you? Is it in his name you were baptized?"[108]

This culpable weakness is often reproduced in our day. Persons otherwise pious carry to excess the esteem and affection

---

[107] Ps. 150:5 (RSV = Ps. 150:6).
[108] 1 Cor. 1:13.

they have for their spiritual directors, exalt without measure their wisdom and holiness, and do not hesitate to depreciate all others. God alone knows the true value of each human being, and we have not the scales of the sanctuary to weigh and compare the respective wisdom and sanctity of this and that person. If you have a good confessor, thank God, and try to render his wisdom useful to you by your docility in allowing yourself to be guided, but do not assume that nobody else has as good a one. To depreciate the merits of some in order to exalt those of others at their expense is a sort of slander, which ought to be all the more feared because it is generally so little recognized.

Zeal must not become bitter

Bear in mind that the zeal that would lead you to undertake works not in conformity with your position, however good and useful they may be in themselves, is always a false one. This is especially true if such cause us interior trouble or annoyance; for the holiest things are infallibly displeasing to God when they do not accord with the duties of our state of life.

"If your zeal is bitter," says St. James, "it is not wisdom descending from on high, but earthly, sensual, diabolical."[109] These words of an apostle should furnish matter for reflection for those persons who, while making profession of piety, are so prone to irritability, so harsh and rude in their manners and language, that they might be taken for angels in church and for demons elsewhere.

[109] James 3:14, 15.

❧

Zeal should make devotion attractive to others

The value and utility of zeal are in proportion to its tolerance and amiability. True zeal is the offspring of charity; it should, then, resemble its mother and show itself like her in all things. "Charity," says St. Paul, "is patient, is kind, is not ambitious and seeketh not her own."[110]

"You should not only be devout and love devotion, but you ought to make your piety useful, agreeable, and charming to everybody. The sick will like your spirituality if they are lovingly consoled by it; your family, if they find that it makes you more thoughtful of their welfare, gentler in everyday affairs, more amiable in reproving, and so on; your husband, if he sees that in proportion as your devotion increases, you become more cordial and tender in your affection for him; your relations and friends, if they find you more forbearing and more ready to comply with their wishes, should these not be contrary to God's will. Briefly, you must try as far as possible to make your devotion attractive to others; that is true zeal."[111]

Never allow your zeal to make you overeager to correct others, says St. Francis de Sales; and when you must do it, remember that the most important thing to consider is the choice of the moment. A caution deferred can be given another time; one given inopportunely is not only fruitless, but, moreover, paralyzes beforehand all the good that might have subsequently been done.

[110] 1 Cor. 13:4, 5.

[111] St. Francis de Sales, Letter to Madame Brulart, May 3, 1604; cf. *Thy Will Be Done*, 46.

Be zealous, therefore, ardently zealous for the salvation of your neighbor, and to further it, make use of whatever means God has placed in your power; but do not exceed these limits nor disquiet yourself about the good you are unable to do, for God can accomplish it through others. In conclusion, zeal, according to the teachings of the Fathers of the Church, should always have truth for its foundation, indulgence for its companion, mildness for its guide, and prudence for its counselor and director.

"I must look upon whatever presents itself each day to be done, in the order of Divine Providence, as the work God wishes me to do and apply myself to it in a manner worthy of Him — that is, with exactness and tranquillity," says Fénelon. "I shall neglect nothing, be anxious about nothing, as it is dangerous either to do God's work negligently or to appropriate it to oneself through self-love and false zeal. When our actions are prompted by our own inclinations, we do them badly, and are pretentious, restless, and anxious to succeed. The glory of God is the pretext that hides the illusion. Self-love disguised as zeal grieves and frets if it cannot succeed.

"O my God, give me the grace to be faithful in action, indifferent to success. My part is to will what Thou willest and to keep myself recollected in Thee amidst all my occupations. Thine it is to give to my feeble efforts such fruit as shall please Thee — none if Thou so wishest."

Chapter Eighteen

⚬

Imitate Christ's meekness

"Blessed are the meek,
for they shall possess the land."
Matthew 5:4

"Learn of me, for I am meek."
Matthew 11:29

❦

Our Lord offers us in His divine Person a model of all the virtues. Meekness, however, is the one that He seems to have wished more particularly to propose for our imitation, since He said, "Learn of me, for I am meek and humble of heart."[112]

Try, therefore, to acquire and always preserve in your soul this Christian virtue and to make all your exterior actions correspond with it. I do not say that you should never have the slightest feeling of irritation, for that would be to expect an impossibility; but you should be attentive to repress these movements and never yield to them voluntarily. It is natural for man to be often assailed by anger, says St. Jerome, but it is peculiar to the Christian not to allow himself to be overcome by it.

A Christian, says St. Bernard, who has no one at hand who gives him occasion to suffer, should seek such a person eagerly and buy him at any price, so that he may have opportunity to practice meekness and patience. If you are not disposed to go to this expense, at least profit of whatever opportunities Divine Providence has given you gratuitously, so that you may accustom yourself to the exercise of these two inestimable virtues.

[112] Matt. 11:29.

How to Love God and Keep His Commandments

An excellent rule to follow is to make a pact with your tongue such as St. Francis de Sales did with his — namely, that the tongue remain silent whenever the feelings are irritated. Otherwise you will begin to speak with the sincere resolution to keep within the bounds of moderation and prudence, but you will never succeed in so doing, because, the bridle once loosened, you will invariably be carried farther than you wish.

⚶

Admonish others peacefully

Reprimand from an angry man can do no good. Reproof is a moral remedy; how would it be possible for you to select and administer this remedy with discernment and prudence, when you yourself are ill and stand in need of both medicine and physician? Wait, therefore, until your soul is at peace, and when you have been restored to calmness, you can speak advantageously. Even when it is your positive duty to administer a rebuke, defer it if possible until you are free from excitement, remembering that for the rebuke to have a salutary effect, both he who gives it and he who receives it must be calm. Without this precaution, the remedy will only aggravate the disease.

When obliged to reprove the fault of another, never fail to pray that God will speak to the person's heart while your words are sounding in his ears.

Observe, however, with St. Gregory the Great and St. Thomas, that if those whom it is your duty to correct abuse your mildness and considerateness, you are then justified in repressing their boldness with vigor and firmness. "Speak to the fool," says the Holy Spirit, "the language that his folly renders necessary, that he may not continue wise in his own eyes."[113] I repeat it: reproof is a remedy, and a remedy must be chosen and proportioned according to the nature and gravity of the evil.

[113] Cf. Prov. 26:5.

Chapter Nineteen

Be charitable in conversations

"Neither do men light a candle and put it under a bushel,
but upon a candlestick, that it may give light to all who are in a house.
Let your light so shine before men that they may see your good works,
and glorify your Father who is in Heaven."

Matthew 5:15-16

"Contend not in words, for it is to no profit,
but to the subverting of the hearers."

2 Timothy 2:14

＊

Conversation should be marked by a gentle and devout pleasantness, and your manner when engaged in it ought to be equable, composed, and gracious. Mildness and cheerfulness make devotion and those who practice it attractive to others. The holy abbot St. Anthony, notwithstanding the extraordinary austerities of his penitential life, always showed such a smiling countenance that no one could look at him without pleasure.

We should be neither too talkative nor too silent; it is as necessary to avoid one extreme as the other. By speaking too much, we expose ourselves to a thousand dangers; by not speaking enough, we are apt to be a restraint upon others, as it makes it seem as though we do not relish their conversation or wished to impress them with our superiority.

"Take great care not to be too critical of conversations in which the rules of devotion are not very exactly observed. In all such matters, it is necessary that charity should govern and enlighten us in order to make us accede to the wishes of our neighbor in whatever is not in any way contrary to the commandments of God."[114]

---

[114] St. Francis de Sales, Letter to Madame Brulart, May 3, 1604; cf. *Thy Will Be Done*, 46.

Do not conclude from this that it is necessary to count your words, as it were, so as to keep your conversation within the proper limits. This would be as puerile a scruple as counting one's steps when walking. A holy spirit of liberty should dominate our conversations and serve to instill into them a gentle and moderate gaiety.

Use prudence when others speak ill of someone

If you hear some evil spoken of your neighbor, do not immediately become alarmed, as the matter may be true and quite public without your having been aware of it. Should you be quite certain that there is calumny or slander in the report, either because the evil told was false or exaggerated or because it was not publicly known, then, according to the place, the circumstances, and your relations toward those present, say with moderation what appears most fitting to justify or excuse your neighbor. Or you may try to turn the conversation into other channels or simply be content to show your disapprobation by an expressive silence. Remember, for the peace of your conscience, that one does not share in the sin of slander unless he give some mark of approbation or encouragement to the person who is guilty of it.

Do not imitate those who are scrupulous enough to imagine that charity obliges them to undertake the defense of every evil mentioned in their presence and to become the self-appointed advocates of whoever it may be that has deserved censure. That which is really wrong cannot be justified, and no one should attempt the fruitless task; and as to the guilty, those who may do harm either through the scandal of their example or the wickedness of their doctrines, it is right that they should be shunned and openly denounced. "To cry out, 'Wolf, wolf,' " says St. Francis de Sales, "is kindness to the sheep."

The regard that we owe our neighbor does not bind us to a politeness that might be construed as an approval or encouragement of his vicious habits. Hence, if it happens that you hear an equivocal jest, a witticism slurring at religion or morals, or anything else that really offends against propriety, be careful not to give, through cowardice and in spite of your conscience, any mark of approbation, even if it is only by one of those half smiles that are often accorded unwillingly and afterward regretted. Flattery, even in the eyes of the world, is one of the most debasing of falsehoods. Not even in the presence of the greatest earthly dignitaries will an honest, upright man sanction with his mouth that which he condemns in his heart. He who sacrifices to vice the rights of truth not only acts unlike a Christian, but renders himself unworthy of the name of man.

⌘

Try to be agreeable

In small social gatherings, try to make yourself agreeable to everybody present and to show to each some little mark of attention, if you can do so without affectation. This may be done either by directly addressing the person or by making a remark that you know will give him occasion to speak of his own accord — draw him out, as the saying is. It was by the charm and urbanity of his conversation that St. Francis de Sales prepared the way for the conversion of numbers of heretics and sinners, and, by imitating him, you will contribute to making piety in the world more attractive. In regard to priests, you should always testify your respect for the sacerdotal dignity quite independently of the individual.

Disputes, sarcasm, bitter language, and intolerance for dissenting opinions, are the scourges of conversation.

Although the following adage comes to us from a pagan philosopher, we might profitably bear it always in mind: "In conversation, we should show deference to our superiors, affability to our equals, and benevolence to our inferiors."

⌘

Do not be aloof

Generally speaking, for those whom God does not call to abandon the world, it is wrong to seclude themselves entirely and to shun all society suited to their position in life. God, who is the source of all virtue, is likewise the author of human society. Let the wicked hide themselves if they will; their absence is no loss to the world. But good people make themselves useful merely by being seen.

Moreover, the world should know that, in order to practice the teachings of the Gospel, it is not necessary to bury oneself in the desert and that those who live for the Creator can likewise live with the creatures He has made according to His own image and likeness. Again, it is good to show that a devout life is neither sad nor austere, but simple, sweet, and easy; that far from being for those in the world an impediment to social relations, it facilitates, perfects, and sanctifies such that the disciples of Jesus Christ can, without becoming worldlings, live in the world and that, in fine, the gospel is the sovereign code of perfection for persons in society as well as for those who have renounced the world.

Fénelon, who perhaps had even greater occasion than St. Francis de Sales to teach men of the world how to lead a Christian life in society, wrote as follows to a person at court:

> You ought not to feel worried, it seems to me, in regard to those diversions in which you cannot avoid taking part. I know there are those who think it necessary that one should lament about everything, and restrain himself continually by trying to excite disgust for the amusements in which he must participate. As for me, I acknowledge that I cannot reconcile myself to this severity. I prefer something more simple, and I believe that God, too, likes it better. When amusements are innocent in themselves and we enter into them to conform to the customs of the state of life in which Providence has placed us, then I believe they are perfectly lawful. It is enough to keep within the bounds of moderation and to remember God's presence. A dry, reserved manner, and conduct not thoroughly ingenuous and obliging, only serve to give a false idea of piety to men of the world who are already too much prejudiced against it, believing that a spiritual life cannot be otherwise than gloomy and morose.[115]

If all confessors agreed in instilling these maxims, which are as important as they are true, many persons who now keep themselves in absolute seclusion and live in a sad and dreary

---

[115] *Christian Perfection*, ch. 2.

solitude would to the edification of their neighbor and the great advantage of religion. The world would thus be disabused of its unjust prejudices against a devout life and those who have embraced it.

⚙

Avoid idleness

Never remain idle except during the time you have allotted to rest or recreation. Idleness begets lassitude, disposes to evil speaking, and gives occasion to the most dangerous temptations.

Chapter Twenty

⚜

Perfect yourself step by step

"Long-standing custom will make resistance,
but by a better habit shall it be subdued."
Imitation of Christ, Bk. 3, ch. 12, no. 5

"To him who shall overcome,
I will grant to sit with me in my throne,
as I also have overcome."
Apocalypse 3:21
(RSV = Revelation 3:21)

❧

We should not undertake to perfect ourselves upon all points at once. Yet, to undertake a little at a time, and to pursue this little with perseverance until one has by degrees brought it to perfection, is a common rule of human prudence.

Resolutions of too general a character — for example, to be always moderate in speech, always patient, chaste, peaceable, and the like — ordinarily do not amount to much and sometimes to nothing at all.

Resolutions as to details ought to be made and carried out one by one, directing them first against our predominant passion. By a predominant passion, we mean the source of that sin to which we most often yield and from which spring the greater number of our faults.

In order to attack it successfully, it is essential to make use of strategy. It must be approached little by little, besieged with great caution as if it were the stronghold of an enemy, and the outposts taken one after another.

For example, if your ruling passion is anger, simply propose to yourself in the beginning never to speak when you feel irritated. Renew this resolution two or three times during the day, and ask God's pardon for every time you have failed against it.

When the results of this first resolution have become a habit, so that you no longer have any difficulty in keeping it, you can take a step forward. Propose, for instance, to repress promptly every thought capable of agitating you, or of arousing interior anger; afterward you can adopt the practice of meeting without annoyance persons who are naturally repugnant to you; then of being able to treat with especial kindness those of whom you have reason to complain. Finally, you will learn to see in all things, even in those most painful to nature, the will of God offering you opportunities to acquire merit; and in those who cause you suffering, only the instruments of this same merciful Providence. You will then no longer think of repulsing or bewailing them, but will bless and thank your divine Savior for having chosen you to bear with Him the burden of His Cross, and for deigning to hold to your lips the precious chalice of His Passion.

It is by this progressive method that you can at length succeed in entirely overcoming your passions and will be able to acquire the virtues you lack. Always begin with what is easiest. Choose at first external acts over which the will has greater control, and in time you can advance from these, little by little, to the most interior and difficult details of the spiritual life.

Resolve, above all, boldly to confess your Faith and to practice it, and let it be known that, in all your actions, your sole desire is to seek the glory of God and the good of your neighbor. Let this profession be made upon occasion in a gentle and modest manner, but firmly and positively, and you will find that subsequently it will be much easier for you to continue what you have thus courageously begun.

Biographical Note

Charles Joseph Quadrupani

(1740-1806)

﹡

Barnabite priest Charles Joseph Quadrupani, born in Lombardy in 1740, served as superior of St. Alessandro's in Milan and as provincial of the Barnabites of Lombardy, but it was for his preaching that he was best known. Beginning in Rome's St. Lorenzo Church in 1771, he dedicated his priesthood to preaching in Italy's major cities, conducting retreats for clergy and laypersons, and offering spiritual direction.

Fr. Quadrupani's writings have been published in an extraordinary number of editions and translations, particularly *How to Love God and Keep His Commandments*. Gathering the wisdom of the Church's most exalted and saintly spiritual directors, he demonstrates the sweetness and peace that come from loving and serving God and presents a practical spiritual program for today's Christians to attain them.

✂

Sophia Institute Press®